SMALL BUSINESS GUIDE TO OBAMACARE:

SOLUTIONS TO THE LOOMING
HEALTH LAW

(WITHOUT THE POLITICS)

CHRISTOPHER J. ENGE

J.D., M.B.A.

ISBN-13: 978-1484907160

ISBN-10: 1484907167

This book is dedicated to everyone who got

back up after being knocked down.

There is not a liberal America and a conservative America - there is the United States of America. There is not a black America and a white America and Latino America and Asian America - there's the United States of America.

– Barack Obama

About the Author

Christopher Enge has practiced and taught business law for over 20 years, advising everyone from mom and pop businesses to startups to global multinationals. A graduate of Stanford Law School and Millikin University, he practiced commercial law in the San Francisco Bay Area and taught law at Skyline and Cañada Colleges. He later moved with his wife Heidi to Frankenmuth, Michigan. He now teaches business law at Saginaw Valley State University, writes, and manages Tozy Tea LLC. In 2011, he earned his MBA from the University of Michigan, Flint, with honors.

You can reach Mr. Enge through his Linkedin profile at http://www.linkedin.com/pub/christopher-enge/3a/8b9/63b or at chrisenge@hotmail.com.

Please visit www.obamacareguide.us.

Table of Contents

Preface

This project began when I went to a local chamber of commerce meeting where the subject was Obamacare. I found myself surrounded by frightened, confused and exasperated businesspeople. So rather than sit back and complain myself, I set out to try to write a guidebook laying out the basic options businesses will have when the law takes full effect in 2014.

Given the subject matter, the challenge was to take a long, complicated law and describe it in a concise manner comprehensible to people who aren't insurance, legal or tax professionals. Mark Twain or Blaise Pascal once said that that he would have written a short letter, but they didn't have time so he wrote a long letter instead. We took the time to try to write a "short letter."

We concentrate on the parts of the law of most importance to businesses and other employers. However, we believe individuals can benefit from this guidebook as well. We first lay out the basic structure and goals of Obamacare. Next, we detail the requirements individuals will face and how the law expects them to meet them. We cover some of Obamacare's consumer protection laws and some of its taxes. Lastly, we get to heart of the matter. We set forth the basic requirements Obamacare imposes on all employers and the options and strategies that should be available.

We try to avoid the political tone of other Obamacare books. Our aim is to provide practical solutions in a straightforward way. In addition, we point out repeatedly that many of the rules we discuss are merely proposed rules. The final rules may turn out to be different so it is critical for you to consult your legal, tax and insurance advisors when you decide what to do for your organization. Planning now based on proposed rules, however, is better than doing no planning at all.

Remember, reading a book is no substitute for sound advice tailored to your situation. As your author but not your lawyer or tax advisor, I can only give the overall view. Only your own lawyer or advisor can give you advice for your situation.

Acknowledgements

I'd like to thank the people who helped with this book. First and foremost, my student research assistant Trevor Ward of Saginaw Valley State University has been of enormous help. In addition, my wife Heidi has patiently allowed me to work on this project. In addition, the following people reviewed early drafts and gave me invaluable guidance and suggestions: Von Schafer, John Tatum, Constance Tatum, Daniel Hahn, Barbara Urbain, and Gerald Naranjo.

I hope you will find this guidebook useful as you try to comply with Obamacare.

May 2013   CHRISTOPHER J. ENGE, J.D., M.B.A

CHAPTER 1

FACING UP TO OBAMACARE

What You Will Need

✦ *Realism*
✦ *Determination*
✦ *An Open Mind*

A. TIME TO GET REAL

You may not like Obamacare. You may have even voted for the other guy—twice. But Obamacare will hit full force in 2014 and 2015. Decisions you make now, in 2013, may limit your choices later. Organizations that prepare, plan and execute the transition well will fare better than those that do not. The mandates, taxes and penalties of Obamacare can potentially ruin a business. This guidebook will help you best manage the transition and perhaps give your organization a competitive advantage.

We set forth practical, hands-on decision-making guidance for business owners under the Patient Protection and Affordable Care Act, sometimes abbreviated PPACA or ACA, but more commonly called Obamacare. Let's start with the name. We use "Obamacare" because that is what most people call the healthcare reform law and even the President has endorsed that name. We mean no disrespect to the law or the President, we seek to make things easier for our readers.

This guidebook follows this basic plan:

Step 1: Help you understand Obamacare's policy goals and the current status, particularly the deadlines for when your organization must act. (Chapters 1-4).

Step 2: What Obamacare requires of you and your employees individually and the means available to satisfy those requirements. You cannot design an attractive employee benefits package without understanding what your employees need to do to comply with the law. (Chapters 5-8).

Step 3: What Obamacare requires employers to do. The rules vary depending on the size of the organization and other factors. (Chapters 9-15).

Step 4: Options and strategies available to employers to best comply with Obamacare. Turn Obamacare into a strategic advantage for your organization. If you don't develop a good strategy, bet your competitors will. (Chapters 16-21).

The government has forced difficult decisions regarding healthcare on every American organization and there is little understandable guidance available. Lawyers and accountants wrote most of the information available for other lawyers and accountants, not laypeople. Other books are more political, basically wishing the new healthcare law would just go away. Our goal is to help you, as a business owner or other employer, find out what information you will need and set forth the options available to you. No nonsense, just practical solutions.

One aspect of Obamacare making it so hard to understand is that many parts of the law interconnect. It's impossible to describe one part of the law without referring to other parts of the law. This means that frequently you will see references to terms described in far more detail later in the book. If you see a term you don't know, we encourage you to look in the glossary. With this kind of book, reading the last part first won't spoil the ending.

A running joke with our students is that law tends to be boring—until we get to a rule that applies to you—then it gets really exciting. Given the subject matter, there is no way to avoid delving into highly technical aspects of the law. Admittedly, this stuff is hard to read. For many readers, it will be easier to use this book as a reference guide rather than trying to read it straight through. The final chapters lay out the available options and strategies for employers. Although we believe it is easier to understand the logic underlying the options with the background concerning the rules, we expect some readers might want to go straight to those chapters.

B. OBAMACARE—A WORK IN PROGRESS

At the outset, it is important to understand Obamacare largely grants powers to federal administrative agencies to make regulations to fill in the details. In this way, Rep. Nancy Pelosi's statement "we have to pass the bill so that you can find out what's in it" is entirely accurate. The Department of Health and Human Services (HHS) and the Internal Revenue Service (IRS) have enormous power to define how Obamacare will apply in specific situations. HHS and the IRS have issued proposed, but in most cases not final, regulations on many subjects and we rely heavily on them in this guidebook. Proposed regulations provide guidance but you will have to check the final regulations to be sure of the final rules.

In addition, Obamacare and the Constitution grant many options to the states and many states have not yet decided what to do. Insurers and medical providers also must decide whether and how to participate in the new health market environment. None of that preparatory work is finished. As of this writing, great uncertainty exists so it is critical for the reader to consult tax, insurance and legal advisors for particular answers to your particular problems. Our hope is that this book points employers in the right direction as best as possible at this time. Each chapter has a reference guide with citations to provisions in

Obamacare, the proposed regulations, and other sources to facilitate further research on your own as well as working with your advisors.

C. OBAMACARE APPLIES TO ALMOST ALL EMPLOYERS

Is this guidebook only for for-profit businesses? No. Obamacare also applies to non-profit organizations like churches, private schools and charities. Even government organizations like state universities and municipal entities fall within Obamacare's coverage. We believe any decision maker from any of these entities can benefit from this guidebook. Also, we believe many individuals will find this guidebook accessible and useful. We address business owners in the text for convenience, even though Obamacare applies to these other types of organizations as well.

D. GOALS OF OBAMACARE

GOAL 1: HEALTH INSURANCE FOR ALL

For a business owner to make good decisions regarding Obamacare, the business owner must understand what the law is trying to achieve. Obamacare has three main goals as well as a lot of subsidiary goals. The primary goal of Obamacare is to make sure every American has health insurance coverage of some sort. Rather than entirely displacing private, employer-based coverage with the government serving as health insurer for everyone (as in Canada) or nearly everyone (as in Britain), Obamacare seeks to make both private and government-sponsored insurance available to more people. The chief means of doing so are (1) vastly expanding Medicaid to millions of people; (2) setting up online exchanges or insurance markets to sell private, government-approved insurance policies to millions of others; and (3) forcing employers to provide coverage to full-time employees.

Why is there so much emphasis on health coverage? Lack of health insurance can financially ruin the family of a person who suffers a catastrophic illness or injury. Even those with insurance face financial calamity once annual or lifetime policy limits are reached. With private insurance, the maximum an insurance company must pay is the policy limit and once it pays that limit it need not pay further. Obamacare seeks to avoid the situation where a seriously ill or injured person is left without coverage.

In addition, hospitals are required to care for the sick and injured regardless of the ability to pay. Therefore, healthcare providers end up providing a great deal of free service, even after wiping out a family's life's savings. Because healthcare providers are ethically and legally required to provide a good deal of care for free, their rates for paying customers are necessarily higher. The idea is that if everyone has some kind of insurance coverage, whether it be private or government provided, families will do better in the face of an emergency and the system overall will function better. Obamacare seeks to get more people to pay into the system through health insurance premiums and higher taxes to address these problems.

Obamacare is designed to solve the lack of coverage problem by forcing many businesses to buy health insurance for their full-time employees or face heavy fines. This is called the employer mandate. At the same time, Obamacare requires almost all individual Americans without employer provided insurance, Medicare or Medicaid to buy insurance, enroll in Medicaid or pay a "penalty tax." This is called the individual mandate. In this guidebook, we go into detail about how the rules work and what options are available.

For many, health insurance is simply too expensive for those who do not qualify for the current Medicaid program. Currently, each state sets its own Medicaid rules within federal guidelines and with federal funding assistance. It will depend on what rules each state sets, but Obamacare funds expanding Medicaid to those with incomes up to 133% of the poverty level (for technical reasons, the effective level will be 138%), which in 2012 was about $15,400 for an individual, about $20,900 for a family of two, and about $31,800 for a family of four.

Although Medicaid historically has shared costs between the state and federal governments, the federal government will pay for

100% of the Obamacare Medicaid expansion from 2014-2016 and 90% thereafter. At the time of this writing, many states have resisted taking the federal money to expand Medicaid, largely because they fear withdrawal of federal funding in future years. See the references at the end of this chapter for a link to a website with a state-by-state Medicaid analysis.

GOAL 2: CONTROL COSTS

Obamacare also seeks to reduce, or at least slow the increase of, the costs of healthcare. It does so by setting strict rules on how much healthcare providers can charge and regulating insurance premiums and payouts. These rules are extremely complex and mostly of interest to healthcare industry professionals and we only cover them in passing in this book.

Obamacare establishes a special independent review board to help control costs. Section 3403 requires establishment of the Independent Payment Advisory Board (IPAB) in 2018.[1] The IPAB will be a government committee set up to find ways to reduce Medicare costs. The IPAB will have 15 members, appointed by the President, confirmed by the Senate and each serving six years. The statute itself limits judicial review of IPAB decisions. The IPAB need not follow normal administrative law procedures and its decisions can only be overridden by 2/3 of both the House and Senate. At this time, it is not clear exactly how powerful the IPAB will be but it looks like the IPAB will have a large say over what is covered and what is not under Medicare, with little chance of override from Congress or the courts.

GOAL 3: CONSUMER PROTECTION AND MINIMUM ESSENTIAL BENEFITS

The third major goal of Obamacare is to provide consumer protections and benefits. This section is a bit of a slog, but you as an employer need to have some familiarity with these rules to be able to comply with Obamacare.

---

1   IPAB is former Gov. Sarah Palin's "death panel."

Although there are hundreds of pages of rules designed to protect consumers, we will mention only some of the most important here. If an employer provides insurance, it must meet these minimum requirements to avoid penalties. This is called "minimum essential benefits."

Obamacare seeks to address the lack of insurance options for those with pre-existing conditions. Just as you cannot buy fire insurance when your house is burning down, private insurance will generally not cover already existing illnesses or injuries. Obamacare mandates coverage to everyone, including those with pre-existing conditions. Of course, this raises the problem of people waiting to buy insurance until they need it, which would ruin private insurance companies. More on that problem later.

Another potentially disastrous problem for someone who becomes seriously ill is that most pre-Obamacare insurance policies had lifetime and annual limits. The insurance policy would cover only up to a certain amount, for example $500,000 or $2,000,000. Once the limit was exhausted, the insurance company had satisfied its obligations and would not pay any more, even if the policyholder still needed more care. We use the past tense, because Obamacare abolishes both annual and lifetime limits.

Obamacare also attempted to address the lack of options for those requiring nursing home care. This effort was abandoned. Medicare generally does not cover long-term care. Obamacare included a government sponsored long-term care program called the Community Living Assistance Services and Supports (CLASS) Act, calling for voluntary payments from employees who could decide whether to enroll in the program. The White House, however, decided not to implement the program, apparently due to doubts about its long-term financial viability. CLASS was finally put to rest when it was repealed in the "Fiscal Cliff" legislation at the beginning of 2013.

Every policy under Obamacare will have to provide "minimum essential benefits," with the exception of certain grandfathered policies as described below. Basically, there will be minimal coverages that every policy will have to have and if they do not, both the employer and the employees will be subject to potentially heavy penalties. HHS has proposed regulations for ten categories of coverage. They are:

1. Ambulatory patient services
2. Emergency services
3. Hospitalization
4. Maternity and newborn care
5. Mental health and substance abuse disorder services
6. Prescription drugs
7. Rehabilitative and habilitative services and devices
8. Laboratory services
9. Preventive and wellness services and chronic disease management
10. Pediatric services, including oral and vision care

Further, each state will have to approve a "benchmark plan," essentially a model for every other plan in the state to follow. There will be limits on how employers and employees share costs, basically protecting employees from having to pay too much.

If a large employer with more than 50 employees provides a plan failing to meet all the minimum benefit requirements it can face a "tax" of $100 per day per employee. Employers must take the time to make sure their insurance plan complies in all respects. The insurance companies are already working to bring their plans into compliance.

In addition to mandated covered items, each policy will need to meet a minimum value test, sometimes called an affordability test. A plan, on average, will need to cover at least 60% of expected cost of care. Basically, each policy will go through a statistical calculation showing that the employer will likely pay on average at least 60% and the employees no more than 40%. The intent of the rule is to limit how much cost the employees bear.

Some plans might qualify for grandfathered status. Much as an existing farm might receive a grandfather exception to a zoning law requiring residential uses, an existing health plan might be able to continue even without full compliance with Obamacare. If a plan was in existence in March 2010 and meets certain other rules, it is exempt from many of Obamacare's requirements. We detail the requirements in Chapter 11.

Business owners need to be aware that the offered plan must provide the required minimum essential benefits and meet an affordability test. If the employer does not offer insurance with minimum essential benefits, the law treats it as if no offer was made at all. A large employer with 50 or more employees AND the employees of any size company could be subject to the Obamacare penalties. Chapter 9 has details about the employer mandate and how to compute the penalties.

REFERENCES AND FURTHER READING

For a more political treatment of Obamacare, see *Beating Obamacare: Your Handbook for Surviving the New Health Care Law* by Betsy McCaughey and *Obamacare Survival Guide: The Affordable Care Act and What It Means for You and Your Healthcare* by Nick J. Tate.

For links to proposed and enacted regulations from Health and Human Services, go to www.hhs.gov.

For links to proposed and enacted regulations from the Internal Revenue Service, go to irs.gov.

For information regarding regulation of health plans and benefits, go to http://www.dol. gov/dol/topic/health-plans/.

For an interactive overview of Obamacare from Blue Cross Blue Shield of Michigan, go to http://www.healthcarereformbasics.com/.

For a map showing what states are planning with regard to the exchanges as of February 2013, go to http://www.washingtonpost.com/blogs/wonkblog/wp/2013/02/18/its-official-the-feds-will-run-most-obamacare-exchanges/.

For current details on each state's Medicaid expansion status, go to http://www.cbpp.org/cms/index.cfm?fa=view&id=3819.

For a description of the ill-fated CLASS program, go to http://blog.heritage.org/2013/03/21/obamacare-at-three-years-one-entitlement-repealed-two-to-go/.

For the proposed regulation relating to minimum essential benefits and actuarial value, see 77 FR 70643, found here http://www.ballardspahr.com/~/media/Files/Alerts/2012-11-28-healthregs-1.pdf.

CHAPTER 2:

OBAMACARE CRITICAL DATES

What You Will Need

✦ *A calendar*

✦ *Periodic review of current status of deadlines, as many have been pushed back.*

You now know the basics of the new law, the major goals and programs. When does the business owner need to start worrying about Obamacare? Probably right now. In many cases, yesterday. Here are some of the most important dates affecting small business. If you don't know what all these programs and terms mean, don't worry, that's what the body of the book is about. In addition, you can check the glossary for many of the technical terms.

March 23, 2010

- Obamacare signed into law
- Grandfather date for existing health plans and policies (See Chapter 11)

September 2010
- 26-year-old children can remain on parents' policies (See Chapter 8)
- No lifetime limits on benefits (See Chapter 8)
- No annual limits on benefits (phase in begins) (See Chapter 8)
- No rescissions of policies absent fraud (See Chapter 8)
- Small business tax credit for businesses under 25 employees (35% of premiums paid) (See Chapter 13)
- Tanning Tax Begins (See Chapter 14)

January 2011
- Health Savings Account (HSA) and Flexible Spending Account (FSA) cannot be used for non-prescription over-the-counter drugs (See Chapter 8)
- W2 must report aggregate cost of employer-sponsored coverage (Check with your accountant)

October 2012
- CLASS long term care program enrollment was to begin but it was repealed (See Chapter 1)

January 2013
- Income tax deduction threshold for medical expenses increases from 7.5% to 10%
- Payroll tax hike
- 3.8% surcharge tax on unearned income goes into effect
- Tax on medical device manufacturers and importers goes into effect (See Chapter 14)
- FSA contribution limited to $2500, adjusted for inflation in future years (See Chapter 8)
- Medical device tax begins (See Chapter 14)

October 2013
- Open enrollment for exchange policies begins (Chapter 7)

March 2013

- Employers must provide written notice of exchanges and potential availability of subsidies to employees (date moved by Dept. of Labor to as yet unknown future date) (See Chapter 4)

January 2014

- Individual mandate penalty tax applies (See Chapter 5)
- Employer mandate takes effect (delayed to 2015) (See Chapter 9)
- Medicaid expansion goes into effect (See Chapter 6)
- Health insurance exchanges open (See Chapter 7)
- Program allowing people under 30 to get catastrophic insurance begins
- Minimum essential health benefits rules apply (See Chapter 9)
- Small business tax credit goes up to 50% (See Chapter 13)
- Total ban on annual limits (See Chapter 8)
- Small Business Health Options Program (SHOP) becomes available (however, the government recently announced delay in full implementation until at least 2015) (See Chapter 7)
- Wellness program rules take effect (See Chapter 5)
- Catastrophic policies become available to individuals under age 30 (See Chapter 7)

January 2015

- Employer mandate enforcement begins
- Anyone who provides minimum essential coverage must report doing so to IRS
- Individual mandate penalty tax increases (See Chapter 5)
- Employer mandate penalty increases (See Chapter 9)
- Basic Health Plan becomes available (was to be 2014, HHS says 2015 at the earliest) (See Chapter 6)

January 2016

- Individual mandate penalty tax increases (See Chapter 6)
- Employer mandate penalty increases (See Chapter 9)

January 2017

- CLASS was supposed to start paying benefits but the program was repealed (See Chapter 1)
- States may open exchanges to large employers under SHOP (See Chapter 7)

January 2018

- Independent Payments Advisory Board (IPAB) becomes effective (See Chapter 1)
- Cadillac plan tax on expensive health insurance plans becomes effective (See Chapter 14)

REFERENCES AND FURTHER READING

For an excellent, detailed timeline for 2013-2014 with citations, see http://www.michbar.org/health/pdfs/timeline.pdf.

Groom Law Group posted a comprehensive timeline complete with citations here http://www.groom.com/media/publication/680_GLG%20 Effective%20Date%20Timeline%20Final.pdf.

For the blog entry announcing the delay in enforcement of the employer mandate, go to http://www.treasury.gov/connect/blog/Pages/Continuing-to-Implement-the-ACA-in-a-Careful-Thoughtful-Manner-.aspx.

CHAPTER 3:

COURTS

What You Will Need
✦ *An Open Mind*

Our Constitution divides power between the federal government and the states. In addition, the Constitution allocates power among Congress, the President, and the courts. The courts are just beginning to have their say. The final shape of the law will depend not only on laws Congress enacts and regulations the executive branch issues, but on how courts rule.

Uncertainty surrounds constitutional questions about Obamacare. An employer does not need to know the details of all these lawsuits, but should be aware that it is unlikely a court will throw out all of Obamacare before it becomes fully effective in 2014 and 2015.

Here is what we know for sure at this point. The individual mandate requiring everyone to buy insurance is an unconstitutional attempt to exercise Congress's power to regulate interstate commerce, but *is a constitutional tax. Nat'l Fed. Of Ind. Bus. v. Sebelius,* 567 U.S. ____ (2012). However, the fines imposed *are not taxes* under other statutes like the Anti-Injunction Act. That bit of legal sleight of hand saved the individual mandate and probably Obamacare in its totality. That is why the government now calls these fines a "penalty tax" and we use that term in this guidebook.

Sebelius also found that Obamacare's expansion of Medicaid coupled with the threat of cutting off all Medicaid funding to states that did not comply was unconstitutional. Each state therefore can choose whether to accept Obamacare's expansion of Medicaid without fear of losing all its Medicaid funding.

Obamacare is an extremely complex law applying to almost every organization in America. Even though it is unlikely a court will deal a fatal blow to Obamacare in its entirety, challenges to specific aspects or specific applications in particular situations could succeed. These include challenges to particular requirements such as forcing employers like Domino's Farms, Hobby Lobby and Catholic organizations to purchase coverage for abortion-inducing drugs and contraceptives despite their religious objections. Other technical challenges are finding their way through the courts, such as whether Obamacare is invalid because it is a tax bill that originated in the Senate or whether the employer mandate is invalid in states with federal exchanges.

The bottom line for a business owner is that there is tremendous uncertainty about who is required to do what. However, we caution against delaying action while hoping for a court ruling to make Obamacare go away as that is highly unlikely.

REFERENCES AND FURTHER READING

The Supreme Court upheld the individual mandate and struck down the "manda-tory" Medicaid expansion in *Nat'l Fed. Of Ind. Bus. v. Sebelius*, 567 U.S. _____ (2012). The opinion with commentary can be found here http://www.scotusblog.com/case-files/cases/national-federation-of-independent-business-v-sebelius/.

The Thomas More Law Center has been handling cases relating to Catholic objections to Obamacare's contraception mandate. Details on those suits can be found at their site http://www.thomasmore.org/.

Pacific Legal Foundation has brought a case challenging Obamacare on the grounds that it is a tax that did not originate in the House of Representatives as required by the Constitution. Details are here http://www.pacificlegal.org/releases/The-election-is-over-but-PLFs-Obamacare-suit-goes-on.

The State of Oklahoma has challenged Obamacare because of defects in the way exchange subsidies are allocated and tax penalties on business enforced. Details are here http://www.cato.org/blog/oklahoma-wins-lawsuit-whole-structure-obamacare-starts-fall-apart.

Further analysis of the lack of subsidies on the federal exchanges http://www.americanbar.org/newsletter/publications/aba_health_esource_home/aba_health_law_esource_0912_sanders.html.

A website collecting Obamacare lawsuits and results from around the country, com-plete with scoreboard and map, is here http://healthcarelawsuits.org/.

For a detailed legal analysis of the lack of subsidies in the federal exchanges problem, go to http://law.case.edu/journals/HealthMatrix/Documents/23HealthMatrix1.5.Article.AdlerFINAL.pdf.

CHAPTER 4:

OBAMACARE—HERE AND THERE

What You Will Need

✦ *If you are in the healthcare industry, find out about incentives and penalties under Obamacare.*

✦ *If you are a member of an Indian tribe, find out what exemptions apply to your personal and business situation.*

✦ *If you sell food or beverages, what nutritional information Obamacare requires you to provide.*

✦ *Policies to avoid or mitigate whistleblower suits.*

✦ *If you are a large employer, compliance with the breastfeeding rules.*

✦ *Pay attention to what disclosures you must make to employees.*

There are many special circumstances that Obamacare addresses. We thought readers would benefit from a chapter collecting some of Obamacare's seemingly random rules. If one of these provisions potentially applies to your situation, you will have to investigate further.

A. HEALTHCARE WORKFORCE

Title V of Obamacare tries to deal with the coming shortage of health-care workers, such as doctors and nurses. It contains a variety of incentives for people to become healthcare professionals. These programs and rules go beyond the scope of this book but we want readers to be aware they exist.

Obamacare also creates causes of action for patients who suffer abuse in healthcare facilities. Basically, patients will be able to sue healthcare providers with facilities that are abusive. If you are in the healthcare industry, you will need to contact your lawyers to get advice on how to avoid lawsuits under these new laws.

B. SPECIAL JURISDICTIONS

Obamacare has many rules that apply to narrow circumstances. For example, Native American tribes are largely exempt and have their own healthcare systems. In addition, U.S. territories have their own special rules. If your organization operates in one of these special jurisdictions you will have to research what rules govern your situation.

C. NUTRITION INFORMATION

If your business sells food or beverages, even from a vending machine, you need to determine whether Obamacare requires special health information labeling. Section 4205 of Obamacare requires labeling in certain circumstances, with the Food and Drug Administration (FDA) filling in the details. The FDA has taken the position that §4205 became effective when Obamacare passed in March 2010, but that full implementation requires further guidance and regulation from the FDA. Companies will need to comply within 6 months of issuance of the final regulations. As of the time of this writing, the FDA was accepting comments but had not issued final regulations.

Here is what we know at this time. Restaurants with more than 20 locations will have to provide caloric information on menus, menu boards, even for drive-throughs. Printed information with other data like fat and sodium content will have to be available on request. Vending machine operators with more than 20 machines will have to provide similar information as well. If you are in a business that might be affected, check the FDA website for more details.

D. WHISTLEBLOWER SUITS

Obamacare also creates new causes of action to support new kinds of lawsuits. One of these new kinds of lawsuits involve whistleblower protections for employees who report violations of the law. Employers will not be able to retaliate against employees who report violations of Obamacare to the authorities. Employers must educate their managers to these rules and adopt policies to ensure compliance.

E. BREASTFEEDING MOTHERS

Large employers, those with 50 or more full-time employees, need to be aware of Obamacare's rules regarding breastfeeding mothers, which became effective in 2010. Large employers will have to provide a reasonable break time for an employee to breastfeed her child for up to one year after the child's birth. In addition, large employers will have to provide a private place other than a bathroom for the mother to breastfeed her child. Employers will still have to comply with state law on this subject if the state law provides for greater employee rights. Check with your legal advisors for regulations applicable to your situation.

F. DISCLOSURES TO EMPLOYEES

Obamacare requires employers to make certain disclosures to employees. Section 1512 requires employers to provide information regarding

(1) the existence of the health insurance exchanges; (2) the potential availability of tax credits for exchange-based policies; and (3) the fact that employees could lose their employer-provided health benefits if they purchase an exchange-based policy. This disclosure was supposed to take place in March 2013, but the Department of Labor has pushed it back to an undisclosed date. You will need to monitor when your organization will have to provide this information to its employees and the exact format and information the government will require.

REFERENCES AND FURTHER READING

For summaries of various provision affecting the healthcare workforce, go to http://www.pascenter.org/reform/#id_35.

For a summary of provisions relating to Native Americans, see http://
www.hsd.state.nm.us/pdf/hcr/38%20Major%20PPACA%20
Provisions%20Related%20to%20Native%20Americans.pdf.

For details of some of the rules in U.S. territories, see http://www.mha-ins.com/
news-updates/more-news-update/january-2013/m.blog/296/hhs-issues-letter-
detailing-standards-and-details-relating-to-exchanges-in-u-s-territories.

For a good discussion of the new food labeling requirements, see http://www.natlaw-
review.com/article/how-many-calories-burger-ppaca-makes-sure-you-know.

A good introduction to the whistleblower lawsuit rules is here http://www.
mondaq.com/unitedstates/x/227324/Whistleblowing/OSHA+Issue
s+Interim+Final+Rule+on+PPACA+Whistleblower+Provision.

A good starting point for the workplace breastfeeding rules is here
https://www.americanbar.org/newsletter/publications/aba_
health_esource_home/Volume7_01_fitzpatrick.html.

For information on the disclosures that were to take place on March 1, 2013
and the government-sanctioned delay, see http://www.hallrender.
com/health_care_law/library/articles/1385/020613_HLB.html.

CHAPTER 5:

THE INDIVIDUAL MANDATE

What You Will Need

+ *Your own annual income*
+ *Awareness of your employees' incomes*
+ *Knowledge of your state's law regarding health exchanges and Medicaid*
+ *Knowledge of applicable exemptions*

A. ALMOST EVERYONE MUST HAVE HEALTH INSURANCE

We now turn our attention to the heart of Obamacare. Obamacare introduces a number of new regulations in the hope of ensuring every American has insurance coverage. The most important may be the requirement that everyone prove they have compliant insurance coverage or pay a penalty tax. A basic understanding of these rules will help business owners make good decisions for their organizations as well as their employees.

As stated above, Obamacare requires insurers to take anyone regardless of pre-existing conditions. The obvious problem is that some people might game the system by buying insurance only after becoming sick or injured. Basically, many people might not pay into the system until they need the benefits from it. Wide-scale freeloading would lead to the system having nowhere near enough money coming in to make it workable.

To address this problem, Obamacare requires everyone, with few exceptions, to buy health insurance, have a job with health insurance, have federal veteran's coverage, or obtain Medicaid, CHIP, or Medicare coverage. People who do not have approved insurance must pay a penalty tax. The individual penalty tax can be hard to compute, but we'll give some examples that should help. Let's start with the basics.

B. COMPUTING THE PENALTY TAX

1. In 2014,[2] the individual penalty tax first takes effect. By 2016, the penalty tax will be at full force. In 2014, the minimum penalty tax is only $95 per person, $285 per family. In 2015, the minimum penalty tax rises to $325 per person, $975 per family. The minimum per person and per family penalty tax will be of $695 per person and $2085 per family in 2016. Uninsured children under the age of 18 face a penalty tax one-half that for an adult in a given year.

2. The alternative penalty tax is based on a percentage of family modified adjusted gross income, with examples shown below. It also phases in and increases over time.

The formula for this income-based penalty tax is:
(Family Income – Income Tax Filing Threshold) * Rate

---

2   As of the time of this writing, despite the delay of enforcement of the employer mandate to 2015 the individual mandate is still to take effect in 2014.

3. The maximum penalty tax is the cost of a bronze insurance policy in that year. In other words, the penalty tax will not exceed the cost of just buying the insurance on the exchanges at the lowest available level. We discuss in detail what a bronze insurance policy is in Chapter 7.

4. For a person or family without qualifying health insurance, the penalty is the greater of either the per-person or income based penalty, with the cost of the bronze policy being the maximum.

The penalty first goes into effect in 2014. The minimum penalty for 2014 is a modest $95 per person or $285 per family. However, as the following chart shows, those with higher incomes but without insurance will face a heavy penalty tax, with a rate of 1.5% of annual income.

Obamacare Penalties For 2014		
Annual Income	Single	Couple
Less than $9500	Exempt	Exempt
$9500 to $15,800	$95	$190
$20,000	$158	$190
$30,000	$308	$190
$40,000	$458	$315
$50,000	$608	$465
$75,000	$983	$840
$100,000	$1,358	$1,215
$125,000	$1,733	$1,590
$150,000	$2,108	$1,965
$175,000	$2,483	$2,340
$200,000	$2,858	$2,715

Assumes Income Tax Filing Threshold
of $9500 for individual and $19,000 for a couple

[3]In 2015, the penalty tax increases to $325 per person or $975 per family, with the income based penalty tax rate increasing to 2.0%.

---

3   We assume an income tax filing threshold of $9500 for an individual and $19,000 for a couple in each year. The maximum penalty, the cost of a bronze plan, is expected to be about $4500 to $5000 per year.

Obamacare Penalties For 2015		
Annual Income	Single	Couple
Less than $9500	Exempt	Exempt
$9500 to $11750	$325	$650
$20,000	$325	$650
$30,000	$410	$650
$40,000	$610	$650
$50,000	$810	$650
$75,000	$1,310	$1,120
$100,000	$1,810	$1,620
$125,000	$2,310	$2,120
$150,000	$2,810	$2,620
$175,000	$3,310	$3,120
$200,000	$3,810	$3,620

Assumes Income Tax Filing Threshold
of $9500 for individual and $19,000 for a couple

By 2016, the full force of the penalty will be in place. The minimum penalty per person will be $695 for adults and $2085 per family. Uninsured children will pay ½, or $347.50. The penalty tax rate increases to 2.5% of income beyond the filing threshold.

The approximate penalties for both individuals and couples in 2016 and into the future are set forth here:

C. EXEMPTIONS FROM PENALTY TAX

As the charts show, the penalty tax can be substantial even for people with modest incomes. Is there a way out for those who desire paying for neither insurance nor a penalty tax? There are a number of exemptions. At this time, it is not clear how these exemptions will be granted and enforced. Will the government interpret the exemptions narrowly or broadly? No one knows. However, the exempt categories are:

Obamacare Penalties For 2016		
Annual Income	**Single**	**Couple**
Less than $9500	Exempt	Exempt
$9500 to $37000	$695	$1,390
$40,000	$763	$1,390
$50,000	$1,013	$1,390
$75,000	$1,638	$1,400
$100,000	$2,263	$2,025
$125,000	$2,888	$2,650
$150,000	$3,513	$3,275
$175,000	$4,138	$3,900
$200,000	$4,763	$4,525

Assumes Income Tax Filing Threshold
of $9500 for individual and $19,000 for a couple

1. Religious conscience exemption. HHS will identify specific religions that object to insurance on moral grounds, such as the Amish or Hudderites. In addition, coverage in a "healthcare sharing ministry" will exempt a person from penalties even if that plan does not meet all the "minimum essential benefits" requirements. Unlike insurance where premiums and coverage are contractual obligations, in a healthcare sharing ministry people pay into the system monthly while voluntarily contributing more when a member has a greater need. These funds are then used to pay for medical needs as they arise. However, if the funds run out because claims are excessive there is no right to sue as there is with a contractual insurance plan.

   Note that this religious exemption to the individual mandate differs from the exemption employers such as the Catholic Church or Hobby Lobby seek. Those organizations seek conscience exemptions from specific provisions of the employer mandate, which of course differs from the individual mandate. They agree they are subject to Obamacare, just not to these specific requirements.

2. Incarcerated individuals. People in state or federal jail or prison are exempt. Presumably, the government already provides healthcare to prisoners.

3. Undocumented aliens. Illegal immigrants cannot benefit from Obamacare and therefore are not compelled to participate. As a large percentage of the uninsured in America are undocumented aliens, Obamacare will fall far short of its promise to insure everyone in America. In addition, Obamacare will not have the benefit of millions of illegal immigrants paying into the system without ever claiming benefits, as is the case with Social Security and Medicare.

4. Required contribution is greater than 8% of household income. People with low incomes are exempt if the bronze policy, net of subsidies, costs more than 8% of their annual household income. For example:

Individual Income:	$45,000
Net Cost of Bronze Policy:	$ 4,000
$45,000 * 8% =	$ 3,600

Because the $4000 cost of a policy exceeds $3600, this person would be exempt from the penalty tax even if the person did not purchase coverage.

5. Person goes without insurance for less than 3 months in a given year. As of the time of this writing, the IRS is still working out the details of this exemption. Under proposed regulations, if a person has a continuous coverage gap of less than 3 months in a given year, there is no penalty tax. Among the issues remaining to be solved are what happens if someone has more than one gap in a year and what happens if a short term gap occurs at the end of the year but totals over 3 months in the next year.

6. Hardship per HHS. HHS has the power to grant hardship exemptions in particular categories of cases. As of this writing, it does not appear HHS has yet defined "hardship."

7. Income below filing threshold. A person making less than $9750 in 2012 does not have to file a federal income tax return. If a person makes less than the equivalent filing threshold in future years, that person is exempt from the penalty tax. It seems likely that most adults of working age falling below the filing threshold would be eligible for Medicaid in states that accept the Medicaid expansion. For those living in states without the Medicaid expansion, some will not be eligible for Medicaid despite extremely low incomes.

8. Members of Indian tribes. Indian tribes, as sovereign states, have their own healthcare system through the Indian Health Service governed largely by the Indian Healthcare Improvement Act and their members are therefore exempt from the penalty tax.

D. ENFORCEMENT OF THE INDIVIDUAL MANDATE

A curious detail is how the government plans to enforce the individual penalty tax. That responsibility falls on the IRS even though HHS makes most of the rules. If you have qualifying insurance, you will file a form saying so. If not, you will calculate a penalty tax and add it to your tax bill.

Here's the weird part. Obamacare limits the IRS's normal enforcement powers. If you do not pay your federal income tax, the IRS can seize your assets and garnish your wages. Obamacare forbids those procedures for collecting the Obamacare penalty tax. It appears the only way the IRS can collect an unpaid penalty tax is to withhold a refund. Many taxpayers may set their exemptions high on their W2 forms to avoid having a refund owing. In other words, it seems the IRS could not enforce the penalty tax against someone with no refund, so it seems likely some people without insurance might avoid the penalty tax by making sure the government owes them nothing at the end of the tax year.

REFERENCES AND FURTHER READING

For a good introduction to the individual mandate with references to the specific sections, go to https://www.bcbsri.com/ BCBSRIWeb/pdf/Individual_Mandate_Fact_Sheet.pdf.

For a concise explanation of the computation of the penalty tax with examples, go to http://www.businessinsider.com/how-much-is-the-obamacare-penalty-tax-2012-7.

For a "crib sheet" on the personal mandate and its exemptions, go to http://www.nfib.com/research-foundation/cribsheets/individual-mandate.

For further information about healthcare sharing ministries, visit http://www.healthcaresharing.org/.

For a summary of proposed regulations regarding the individual mandate, including coverage gaps, minimum essential coverage, and the individual penalty tax, go to http://www.towerswatson.com/en/Insights/Newsletters/Americas/ health-care-reform-bulletin/2013/PPACA-Guidance-Individual-Mandate-Minimum-Essential-Coverage-Family-Members-Subsidy-Eligibility.

For an excellent analysis by two law professors of the limitations on the IRS's normal enforcement powers, go to http://taxprof.typepad.com/files/135tn1633-1.pdf.

For final IRS regulations regarding shared responsibility requirements (taxes and penalties), go to For IRS regulations regarding the individual mandate shared responsibility provisions (taxes and penalties), go to http:// www.irs.gov/PUP/newsroom/REG-148500-12%20FR.pdf.

CHAPTER 6

EXPANSION OF MEDICAID AND THE BASIC HEALTH PLAN

What You Will Need

✦ *Knowledge of state law where you have employees*
✦ *Knowledge of income level of employees*

A. MEDICAID AVAILABLE TO MANY MORE PEOPLE

We now know that the penalty tax is supposed to force people to obtain health insurance. How can they satisfy that requirement? First, we look at the Medicaid expansion. Medicaid is the health insurer of last resort for the poor in America. Medicaid is run by the states with funding help from the federal government. Generally, in most states, Medicaid covers only low-income people with children. Under Obamacare, Medicaid expands to cover people with incomes up to 138% of the poverty line, about $15,400 per year for an individual and $31,809 for a family of four in 2012 without regard to whether they have children. A large number of people with jobs should be eligible for Medicaid after the expansion. About half of the currently 30 million uninsured Americans are expected to eventually gain coverage through the Medicaid expansion although there is no way to know for sure.

The great uncertainty here is whether states will go along with the federal plan. Although the federal government is committing to funding the entire expansion for people newly eligible for Medicaid in the initial years (2014-2016) and 90% thereafter, many states have expressed concern about what happens if the federal government withdraws funding in the future. In addition, there may be hidden costs to states arising from the fact that not everyone currently eligible for Medicaid has applied for Medicaid. Some governors have expressed concern about the impact on their budgets when people currently uninsured but eligible for Medicaid signing up for Medicaid because of the individual mandate, a cost not reimbursed as part of the Obamacare expansion.

In *Nat'l Fed. of Ind. Bus. v. Sebelius*, more than half the states challenged the Medicaid expansion–and won. Each state therefore has the right to choose whether to expand Medicaid. Readers will have to check local state law to find out what has happened by 2014. At the end of this chapter you will find a link to a webpage tracking every state's current Medicaid expansion status.

B. BASIC HEALTH PLAN OPTION

Another option that might be available to some people is the Basic Health Plan. Each state must decide whether it will have the Basic Health Plan. It will provide coverage to those with incomes between 133% and 200% of the federal poverty level. The Basic Health Plan could be an option for those with incomes too high for Medicaid, even after the Obamacare expansion.

The Basic Health Plan, if a state chooses to have it, will have the same essential benefits as policies in the exchanges. However, those taking the Basic Health Plan cannot get subsidies for an exchange plan.

As of this writing, states are concentrating on the Medicaid expansion. The federal government is concentrating on the exchanges and other regulations. HHS has announced it will delay implementation of the Basic Health Plan until at least 2015.

REFERENCES AND FURTHER READING

For an analysis of the Medicaid expansion, go to http://www.healthcarereform-magazine.com/article/health-reform-and-medicaid-expansion.html.

For a map with what each state is doing with regard to Medicaid as well as links to recent articles, go to http://www.advisory.com/Daily-Briefing/2012/11/09/MedicaidMap.

Another website collecting the status of each state with regard to Medicaid is here http://www.cbpp.org/cms/index.cfm?fa=view&id=3819.

For a discussion of the political pressures involved in the Medicaid expansion, see http://www.economist.com/news/united-states/21572813-more-governors-will-expand-medicaid-now-they-must-improve-it-offer-they-cant-refuse.

Frontline recently ran a story regarding the difficulties faced by those falling between Medicaid's coverages . http://www.pbs.org/wgbh/pages/frontline/health-science-technology/dollars-and-dentists/when-the-dentist-wont-see-you/

For a discussion of the Basic Health Plan and the government announced delay, see http://capsules.kaiserhealthnews.org/?p=16689.

CHAPTER 7

HEALTH INSURANCE EXCHANGES

What You Will Need

✦ *Your state exchange's web address or the federal exchange web address*

✦ *Consideration of whether exchange policies are a good option for you and your employees*

A. WHAT'S A HEALTHCARE EXCHANGE?

The most visible new feature will be online healthcare exchanges providing options for insurance policies. Although no Obamacare exchanges are up and running yet, the basic idea seems to be to mimic travel websites like Orbitz or Travelocity. The customer inputs information, the website generates the options, and the customer picks the best policy. Competition in the exchanges among private insurers should keep prices down and costs under control, at least in theory. The schedule calls for open enrollment for exchange policies to begin in October 2013.

Exchanges will not be just for individuals but for organizations as well. Obamacare introduces a program called the Small Business Health Options Program (SHOP). In 2014, small businesses will be able to purchase policies for their employees on exchanges. Although originally SHOP was to provide a variety of competitive choices to employees, the government recently announced there will be only one option in 2014 and implementation of a choice of plans will be delayed until at least 2015. In 2017, states will have the option of opening their exchanges to larger companies.

The exchanges will have open enrollment periods, with HHS determining the particular dates. This means that new customers will be able to buy insurance only during the open enrollment period. Open enrollment will begin in October 2013, but we do not know the annual periods after that. The purpose of open enrollment periods is to encourage people to purchase insurance before they are sick or injured.

The only two states with pre-Obamacare exchanges are Utah and Massachusetts. By 2014, each state is expected to have its own exchange, with a federal exchange for states that either can't or won't set up their own exchanges. To date, few states have moved forward with exchanges. Some states, such as Michigan, have suggested a "hybrid" exchange run partly by the state and partly by the federal government. Negotiations are ongoing but the federal government has expressed interest in pursuing hybrid exchanges. It appears, however, the federal government will carry a heavier load than previously anticipated as many states balk at setting up exchanges. We provide a link at the end of the chapter to a website that tracks what each state is doing with regard to the exchanges.

B. ELIGIBILITY FOR EXCHANGE TAX CREDITS

Obamacare provides subsidies to help people with modest incomes buy policies on the exchange. The government will issue tax credits, sometimes called subsidies, to eligible people based on their incomes. Who will be eligible for exchange subsidies? Here's the list:

1. Citizens and legal residents of the United States with modified adjusted gross incomes between 100% and 400% of the federal poverty level who purchase insurance through an exchange. In 2012 these levels would be about $11,170 to $44,680 for an individual and $23,050 to $92,200 for a family of four.

2. People offered employer-based coverage with an actuarial value less than 60% or not offered employer-based coverage at all. What this means is that the government has a complex calculation for determining whether a policy an employer offers is affordable. If an offered policy is unaffordable, the employee can purchase a policy on an exchange and obtain a subsidy.

3. People offered employer-based coverage where the employee's share is more than 9.5% of family income.

4. Married couples must file a joint return to be eligible for a subsidy.[4]

Who is not eligible?
1. People eligible for public coverage. This means that if you are eligible for Medicaid or Medicare, if you want to buy a policy on an exchange you will have to pay the full cost. In addition, veterans with access to Tricare for Life or veteran's healthcare coverage under Chapter 17 of Title 38 are not eligible for subsidies. Lastly, Peace Corps volunteers with access to that program's health insurance are not eligible for Obamacare subsidies.

---

4   Section 1401(c)(1)(C) requires married couples to file jointly to be able to claim the exchange tax credit. This rule apparently tries to limit triggering a greater subsidy where one spouse earns a lot more than the other. In addition, it avoids the problem of assigning the children to the "poor" spouse to get a credit for them. This rule creates an incentive for couples in that situation to remain unmarried or divorce to obtain potentially large tax credits.

2. People offered compliant insurance through an employer.

3. People with incomes less than 100% of the federal poverty level in states without Medicaid expansion. Yes, there is a gap in the law where low-income people could be eligible for neither Medicaid nor a subsidy yet still be subject to the individual mandate.

C. DEFINING INCOME

An issue gaining some but not a lot of attention so far is how income is defined under Obamacare. Pop quiz: What is the latest information the government will have about people's income on January 1, 2014? Five points if you said the *2012* tax return. Most people will not file their 2013 returns until April 2014, making the 2012 return the most recent filing available at the start of 2014. Which year's income determines eligibility for Medicaid or the exchange subsidies? *2014*. As we will see, this discrepancy creates problems for many people and the government is just now trying to address them.

For eligibility for both Medicaid and the premium credits on the exchanges, Obamacare looks at "Modified Adjusted Gross Income" (MAGI). Your Adjusted Gross Income appears at lines 37 on your 1040 income tax form. To get MAGI, you will need to subtract certain income items from the Adjusted Gross Income. We can only hope the IRS will provide a relatively easy way of performing that calculation.

MAGI includes not only wages and salaries, but also tips, taxable interest, dividends, business income and capital gains. Also included are retirement income items such as annuities, Social Security payments, and some pensions.

A big problem for business owners posed by these rules is that their income can vary greatly. Most people will not know their MAGI for 2014 until they complete their taxes in the spring of 2015. A small startup company, or any business for that matter, might suffer losses, potentially leaving the owner below 100% of the federal poverty level and therefore ineligible for the subsidies. Even if the owner can afford the insurance from savings, there will be no subsidy available. If a business owner lives in a state that expands Medicaid, that option could be available. If not, the business owner who has a bad year might be stuck paying full price for exchange-based policies.

The IRS regulations appear to provide relief for this situation. If a person gets an exchange policy and subsidy based on estimated income above 100% of the federal poverty line but ends up earning less, the IRS has said such a person will not have to pay the subsidy back.

The IRS's bending of the rules probably makes sense when understood against the backdrop of Obamacare's main purposes. A common situation where someone's income might drop below the estimated amount would be where a person suffers an injury or illness and can no longer work for an extended period of time. That would seem to be exactly the kind of situation where Obamacare is supposed to help. Penalizing such a person by requiring the refunding of a subsidy would seem perverse in the extreme.

The problem works the other way around as well. Someone could sign up for Medicaid or exchange-based policy based on their estimated wages, but then have other income push them over the eligibility thresholds. A business could have a good year, resulting in ineligibility for a planned tax credit. The IRS regulations require someone who received a subsidy but ends up going over 400% of the poverty level to refund the entire subsidy.

What if someone's income is different from the estimate at the time of receiving the subsidy, but the income ends up a bit higher or lower but still qualifies for the subsidy? At the time of this writing, the possible solution being discussed is limiting how much someone who underestimates income has to pay back from a subsidy that turns out to be too large. For example, a family of four making between $47,000 and $70,000 would face a maximum payback amount of $2500, even if the excess subsidy they received exceeds $2500. Even under that proposal, however, if a person receives a subsidy but it turns out that person made too much to be eligible, the person has to return the entire subsidy. If a person is entitled to a bigger subsidy, that person will receive the extra amount as a tax refund.

At this time, all we can advise is for you to be very careful when estimating your income. In addition, you may be able to find ways to control your income more precisely. For example, you should factor in the impact on the Obamacare credits when you take a capital gain or loss. Don't forget investment income when estimating your MAGI for the exchange.

Business owners may be able to manage their income to ensure eligibility for a subsidy or Medicaid. Pass through entities like partnerships, S corporations, and limited liability companies lead to variations in business income causing variations in personal income. A solution that might help would be to organize your business as a C corporation and pay yourself a salary, but that would subject the company to corporate income tax. That strategy could help smooth out fluctuations in your personal income from year to year. In addition, managing the timing of payments of bills or collections of receivables at the end of the year could help achieve the desired income.

D. EXCHANGE COST PROJECTIONS

Assuming someone, somewhere establishes the exchanges, what should we expect? First, there will be four plan levels—platinum, gold, silver and bronze. The difference is not in what diseases the policies cover or the kinds of treatments offered, but rather in what percentage of costs the plan is expected to cover. The more the policy pays for, the more it will cost.

For many, the policies on the exchanges will be a good deal. Based on the University of California Berkeley Labor Center's calculator[5],

---

5   There are some big assumptions behind these numbers. They include:

1. Assumes the state accepts the full 133% + 5% Medicaid expansion, but does not account for state-specific rules on Medicaid and CHIP

2. Assumes no affordable offer

3. If income above 400% of FPL, the policyholder pays full premium. Premium cost is based on the project cost of a silver (70%) policy.

4. CBO's estimates of premiums, adjusted for inflation.

5. Uses formula based on statute for calculating subsidies.

Plan	Policy's Expected Share	Insured's Expected Share
Bronze	60%	40%
Silver	70%	30%
Gold	80%	20%
Platinum	90%	10%

which builds in forecasted premiums from the Congressional Budget Office (CBO), here are some common scenarios based on 2016 numbers. The first column shows income, the second the penalty tax, and the others show expected out of pocket costs of a silver policy at various ages. These tables are based on projections and are presented here, as illustrations of approximately what the costs are likely to be.

Annual Penalty Compared to Annual Premium (2016)

Annual Penalty for Individual Compared to Annual Premium Net of Subsidies (2016)				
Annual Income	Single Penalty	Single (25)	Single (40)	Single (60)
Up to $15,000	$695	Medicaid	Medicaid	Medicaid
$20,000	$695	$1,020	$1,020	$1,020
$30,000	$695	$2,508	$2,508	$2,508
$40,000	$763	$3,468	$3,804	$3,804
$50,000	$1,013	$3,468	$4416	$9,384
$75,000	$1,638	$3,468	$4,416	$9,384
$100,000	$2,263	$3,468	$4,416	$9,384
$125,000	$2,888	$3,468	$4,416	$9,384
$150,000	$3,513	$3,468	$4,416	$9,384
$175,000	$4,138	$3,468	$4,416	$9,384
$200,000	$4,763	$3,468	$4,416	$9,384

Premium projections from U.C. Berkley Labor Center Calculator
http://laborcenter.berkeley.edu/healthpolicy/calculator/

Annual Penalty for Couple Compared to Annual Premium Net of Subsidies (2016)			
Annual Income	Couple Penalty	Couple (40)	Couple (60)
Up to $15,000	$1,390	Medicaid	Medicaid
$20,000	$1,390	Medicaid	Medicaid
$30,000	$1,390	$1,800	$1,800
$40,000	$1,390	$3,312	$3,312
$50,000	$1,390	$4,752	$4,752
$75,000	$1,400	$8,832	$18,768
$100,000	$2,025	$8,832	$18,768
$125,000	$2,650	$8,832	$18,768
$150,000	$3,275	$8,832	$18,768
$175,000	$3,900	$8,832	$18,768
$200,000	$4,525	$8,832	$18,768

Premium projections from U.C. Berkley Labor Center Calculator
http://laborcenter.berkeley.edu/healthpolicy/calculator/

In many cases, it is a lot cheaper to simply pay the penalty. That of course assumes no one gets sick or injured. However, it would not be surprising if many people, especially those with already modest incomes, do not feel compelled to purchase insurance. Some will just buy insurance when they need it.

In addition, the cost of insurance increases dramatically once someone makes enough that the subsidy is not available. Note the extreme increases in the cost of insurance once annual income exceeds $40,000 to $50,000. Given how much the loss of subsidy could cost, if you are close to the borderline you must carefully track all your components of modified adjusted gross income; not just wages and business income, but also investment and capital gains income.

Of course, there is a big potential downside to not having insurance. Obamacare requires insurers to accept and pay for pre-existing *conditions*. The law does not require insurers to pay pre-existing *bills*. Even a short hospital stay after an unexpected accident can cost a fortune. HHS will impose open enrollment periods for the exchanges, meaning that a sick or injured person would have to wait until the next open enrollment period to buy insurance. It is possible that large costs could accrue before the patient obtains insurance. Saving a little now could cost a lot later, so we caution against playing the "wait until we need it" game.

Here's something that is not obvious. Offering affordable insurance to a low paid worker may not be in the worker's best interest. How? Here's an example:

Worker's Income (Single, Age 40, 2016)	$20,000
Offered Policy Cost to Worker	$1800
9% of Income	$1800
Subsidized Cost of Silver Exchange Policy	$1068
Unsubsidized Cost of Silver Exchange Policy	$4548

Because the offer costs 9% of the worker's income, it is "affordable" within the meaning of Obamacare. That worker is now ineligible to buy a silver policy on the exchange costing $1068 net of subsidies under our assumptions. The same silver policy, under our assumptions, will now cost over $4500 on the exchange. The worker will probably accept the employer's offer, even though it costs nearly double what the worker would have paid on the exchange if no affordable offer had been made. If you run an organization with a lot of low-income employees, you need to consider carefully whether offering insurance helps them or hurts them.

E. CATASTROPHIC POLICY FOR YOUNG PEOPLE

In addition to the bronze-platinum plans, people under the age of 30 who have no affordable insurance option will have the option of a high deductible catastrophic plan. If you are under 30, you should explore this option in 2014 as a potentially less expensive way to go.

REFERENCES AND FURTHER READING

For an explanation of the new health insurance market and exchanges
from the government's point of view, go to http://www.
healthcare.gov/marketplace/about/index.html.

For an explanation of SHOP and other issues important to small business, go to
http://www.healthcare.gov/marketplace/small-businesses/index.html.

For information on the SHOP implementation delay, go to http://
ebn.benefitnews.com/news/ppaca-small-business-insurance-
market-delayed-year-bloomberg-2732151-1.html.

For a map showing what states are planning with regard to the exchanges as of
February 2013, go to http://www.washingtonpost.com/blogs/wonkblog/
wp/2013/02/18/its-official-the-feds-will-run-most-obamacare-exchanges/.

To see examples of existing health insurance exchanges, go to Utah's
at http://www.exchange.utah.gov/ or Massachusetts' at https://
www.mahealthconnector.org/portal/site/connector.

For a discussion of federal state partnership hybrid exchanges, go to http://
www.californiahealthline.org/road-to-reform/2013/path-to-part-
nership-more-states-opt-for-hhs-hybrid-exchanges.aspx.

For a good discussion of the subsidy eligibility and calculation rules, go
to http://www.kff.org/healthreform/upload/7962-02.pdf.

A news article regarding the difficulties of computing income for purpose
of granting subsidies can be found here http://washington.cbslo-
cal.com/2013/04/02/millions-could-get-surprise-tax-bills-under-
obamacare-if-they-dont-accurately-project-their-income/3/.

If you would like to estimate your own costs at the exchanges and to see how we computed
the graphs above, go to http://laborcenter.berkeley.edu/healthpolicy/calculator/.

For a discussion of the Obamacare's anti-discrimination rules, go to http://
www.martindale.com/members/Article_Atachment.aspx?od=20
864&id=1562352&filename=asr-1562400.PPACA.pdf.

For some of the final IRS regulations regarding the estimation of income problem,
go to http://www.gpo.gov/fdsys/pkg/FR-2012-05-23/pdf/2012-12421.pdf.

CHAPTER 8:

CONSUMER PROTECTION

What You Will Need

+ *Confirm your plan meets Obamacare requirements*
+ *Determine actuarial value of plan*
+ *Check with insurance provider regarding HSA and FSA plans*

Obamacare imposes new rules on insurance companies that are intended to expand coverage. Many small business owners obtain their own coverage so these rules will be crucial for them. Also, for business owners who now provide healthcare coverage it will be critical to understand the options available to employees if the company reduces or eliminates coverage.

A. RESTRICTED UNDERWRITING RULES

For most kinds of insurance, the insurance company uses information from the prospective insured to gauge the risk of a particular policy, a process called underwriting. If there is more risk of loss, the insurer charges more or might even decline to issue a policy. Conversely, for low risk policies insurance companies will charge less. That is why auto insurers ask about driving records, type of car, and age of the driver. A 20-year-old man with a history of accidents, drunk driving arrests and speeding tickets in his Corvette is more likely to have an accident than a middle-aged woman with no accidents or violations in a station wagon.

Health insurers under Obamacare are extremely limited in what they can consider when they make underwriting decisions. When setting rates, health insurers may only consider (1) the age of the person; (2) whether the person uses tobacco; (3) geography (i.e. people who live in expensive areas pay more); and (4) size of the family for a family policy. It is unlawful discrimination for an insurer to consider any other factor. Gender, weight, and claims history may no longer be considered.

People with pre-existing conditions can no longer be turned away. The intent is to avoid the situations where people lose their insurance coverage and then suffer a long-term illness or injury, sometimes a financial catastrophe for many families.

Another rule expanding coverage requires insurers to include children of policyholders up to the age of 26 as of September 2010. For college students and other young adults with jobs that do not provide coverage, this provides a route to coverage not previously available.

B. ABOLITION OF LIFETIME AND ANNUAL LIMITS

Obamacare also abolishes lifetime and annual coverage limits. Prior to Obamacare, most insurance policies had limits on how much can be paid out during an insured's lifetime or during a policy year. For the unfortunate person with an illness or injury requiring long-term expensive care, the exhaustion of either policy limit can be ruinous. Moreover, exhaustion of the limits can lead to reduced healthcare, impacting actual care decisions. As of 2014, Obamacare abolishes annual and lifetime limits for all plans, including grandfathered plans.

C. LIMITS ON ADMINISTRATIVE EXPENSES

Obamacare also sets a limit on the ratio of administrative expenses to healthcare payments. The idea is that premium dollars should go to healthcare, not overhead. If the amount of claims paid is too low relative to premiums, then the insurance company has to refund part of the premiums.

As a business owner, you do not need to get too bogged down in the mathematics, but here are the basics. If an insurer pays out too little on claims, it must issue refunds to its policyholders. Sometimes this is called the 80/20 rule. At least 80% of premiums must go to benefits and no more than 20% can go to administration and overhead.

D. NO RESCISSIONS ABSENT FRAUD

A rescission is a legal remedy for a contract dispute where the court cancels the contract and puts the parties in the position they would have been in if there had never been a contract. A common rescission scenario would be where someone made a misstatement on an insurance application. Basically, the insurance company says we would not have issued the policy if we had known the truth so it is not fair to hold us to the contract. Although the traditional rule is that any material misstatement could result in rescission, Obamacare requires the proof of actual fraud or intentional misrepresentation.

E. IMPACT ON HEALTH SAVINGS ACCOUNTS AND HIGH-DEDUCTIBLE PLANS

Many small businesspeople have found an affordable approach to healthcare by coupling a high deductible insurance policy with a Health Savings Account. Contributions to the account are tax deductible, much like an IRA. The funds can only be withdrawn for health purposes. Because the policy has a high deductible, it kicks in when there is a more serious need and regular items like annual checkups, routine doctor visits, and prescriptions are paid through the Health Savings Account.

Obamacare makes only two direct changes, but there are several indirect changes that could make Health Savings Accounts unworkable. The first direct change is that Health Savings Account funds can only be used for over the counter drugs with a doctor's prescription. Second, the early withdrawal penalty has increased from 10% to 20%. In this context, early withdrawal means the funds did not go toward a legitimate medical expense.

To work around these rules is relatively easy: get a prescription for over the counter drugs if they are expensive enough to make it worth the trouble and do not withdraw from your Health Savings Account early unless you absolutely must.

That does not sound too bad, but Health Savings Accounts and high deductible plans might not survive Obamacare. Required preventative services, which would have been paid for through the account, are now required in the policy and will be paid for through premiums. In addition, the required essential benefits expand coverage leading to likely premium increases. The medical loss ratios might also fail to meet Obamacare's 80/20 rule.

One rule we know for certain is that the maximum deductible in 2014 will be $2000/individual and $4000/family, lower than many high deductible plans. Lower deductibles require higher premiums because the insurer's obligation to pay arises sooner and more frequently. It remains to be seen how high deductible plans will fare under the 2014 actuarial value (affordability) and out of pocket expense rules (80/20 rule).

Perhaps the coup de grace will be in 2018 when the Cadillac plan tax begins (that tax is explained in more detail in Chapter 14). The Cadillac plan tax imposes a 40% tax on health plans that cost more than a pre-determined limit. At the time of this writing, not just the premium but also contributions to a Health Savings Account will count toward the Cadillac tax cap, which may make many of these plans totally unaffordable. However, these proposed rules are not final so if you have an HSA you will need to check the final rules.

F. IMPACT ON FLEXIBLE SPENDING ACCOUNTS

Flexible Spending Accounts are in some ways similar but in many ways very different from Health Savings Accounts. Flexible Spending Accounts allow an employee to set aside funds from compensation on a pre-tax basis for medical expenses. As time goes by, the employee uses the funds to pay for medical expenses as the need arises.

Unlike a Health Savings Account, however, Flexible Spending Accounts are a "use it or lose it" proposition. If money remains in the account at the end of the year, the employee loses it. Prior to Obamacare, contributions to Flexible Spending Accounts was unlimited, with the "use it or lose it" rule punishing those who set aside too much. Under Obamacare, the limit on contributions will be $2500 per year.

In addition, similar to Health Savings Accounts, the penalty for non-allowed purchases increases from 10% to 20%. Moreover, the prohibition on the purchase of non-prescription over the counter drugs also applies to Flexible Spending Accounts. Again, it is hard to predict the long-term viability of Flexible Spending Accounts.

REFERENCES AND FURTHER READING

For an overview of the underwriting rules, ban on annual limits and rescissions, and other rating considerations under Obamacare, go to http://publications.milliman.com/publications/healthreform/pdfs/rating-underwriting-under-new.pdf.

For a brief discussion of the 80/20 rule, go to http://www.imctr.com/Content.aspx?id=2484.

For further details about the proposed rules regarding Health Savings accounts, go to http://www.hallrender.com/health_care_law/library/articles/1157/060612HLB4.html.

For a discussion of the Flexible Savings Account proposed rules, go to http://www.natlawreview.com/article/recent-ppaca-guidance-new-2500-health-fsa-limit.

CHAPTER 9:

EMPLOYER MANDATE

What You Will Need

+ *Number of full-time employees in each month*

+ *Hours worked per week by part-time employees*

+ *Careful analysis of status of seasonal, part-time, temporary workers and independent contractors*

+ *What health coverage is currently offered and dates the plan runs*

+ *Pay levels for not just employees but family income as well[6]*

+ *What plan was in place in March 2010*

+ *Length of measuring periods and stability period*

+ *Excellent records of how much each employee works, including salaried employees*

+ *As much clarity as possible as to the status of each worker*

---

6   Maybe. IRS is creating a safe harbor based on an employee's W2 income, not family income as stated in the statute. This proposed safe harbor is explained below.

A. OVERVIEW OF EMPLOYER MANDATE

Obamacare requires all employers with more than 50 full-time employees to offer compliant insurance or pay a "shared responsibility payment," which we will call a "ShaRP," if a full-time employee obtains a subsidy for a policy on an exchange.[7] Part-time workers can also count toward the 50-employee threshold. We detail this calculation below.

Some may wonder whether Obamacare's employer mandate only applies to private, for-profit businesses. The answer is that the Obamacare employer mandate broadly applies to employers, including not-for-profits and government entities. It is possible a church, charity or even local public school district could end up having to offer insurance or pay a penalty. The only exception of which we are aware is organizations owned by members of Indian tribes.

Let's say a large employer fails to offer required insurance and an employee goes to the exchange and receives a subsidy. What is the penalty? The employer mandate penalty can really be divided into two separate rules. Some commentators refer to these rules as the "Big Risk Rule" and the "Small Risk Rule." The Big Risk Rule applies when an employer fails to offer insurance at all to employees entitled to an offer. The Small Risk Rule applies if an employer makes an offer deemed "unaffordable" to a particular employee, meaning the policy costs too much relative to the employee's income.

Big Risk Rule (Obligation to Offer Insurance): The IRS has proposed and will likely approve a more lenient rule than Obamacare itself requires, calling for offers to only 95% of full-time employees as opposed to all of them as the statute requires. If the employer makes an offer of insurance to less than 95% of its full-time employees, then it pays a penalty based on all its employees ($2000 * (Full-time Employees – 30)). The formula essentially gives a break for the first 30 employees.

---

7   The statute calls for the employer mandate to take effect in 2014, but the government announced it will delay enforcement of the penalties and reporting requirements until 2015.

Big Risk Rule Example

Number of Full-Time Employees	100
Maximum Number Not Offered Insurance	5
Actual Number Not Offered Insurance	6-100
Number Who Get an Exchange Subsidy	1 or more

Penalty = $2000 * (100-30) = $140,000

Small Risk Rule (Failure to Offer Affordable Insurance): If the employer, on the other hand, makes an offer of insurance that is unaffordable to a full-time employee who then gets an exchange subsidy, the employer only pays $3000 for the one employee.

Small Risk Rule Example

Number of Full-Time Employees	100
Number Not Given an Affordable Offer	1
Number Who Get an Exchange Subsidy	1

Penalty = $3000 * (1) = $3,000

Because an employee obtaining a subsidy for an exchange policy triggers the ShaRP, some employers might be tempted to take action against an employee who did so. Employers need to be aware that employees will have a protected right to buy insurance on the exchanges. An employee will be able to sue an employer who discriminates or retaliates against an employee for buying a policy on the exchange.

The strategy response seems to be to err on the side of making offers to full-time employees, even if the offer is unaffordable within the meaning of Obamacare. If the employer offers affordable insurance to all its full-time employees, there is no penalty. However, the penalty for failing to offer insurance at all is potentially much higher than the penalty for failing to offer affordable insurance. A simple example illustrates this point well.

Total Employees	100
Class A (Insured) Employees	95
Class B (Uninsured) Employees	5

At this point, under the IRS's proposed rules the organization is not penalized because it offers insurance to 95% of its full-time employees and is in compliance with the Big Risk Rule. Suppose it decides to hire another Class B employee and does not offer insurance? The company now violates the Big Risk Rule by falling below 95% and must pay a penalty based on the entire workforce (101-30) * $2000 = $142,000.

The better course of action is to make an unaffordable offer to the new employee, while pointing out a better deal may exist on the exchange. If the employee declines the offer and buys insurance on the exchange, the penalty is only $3000 under the Small Risk Rule, which is a lot less than $142,000. Although there are some risks to this strategy and you must speak to your tax and legal advisors before trying it, we wanted our readers to be aware of the option.

B. HOW TO COUNT EMPLOYERS

If an employer has 50 or more full-time employees, then the employer is considered an "applicable large employer" (which we shorten to "large employer"). It may not be obvious, but we first need to count how many employers there are. For most organizations, it will be easy to see there is one employer. However, the IRS will likely apply the same kind of rules for related companies and companies with common ownership that are used in calculating pension requirements or even the income tax to avoid gamesmanship on the part of business owners.

For example, the "Mississippi Christmas Tree" was a scheme to increase farm subsidies by dividing a farm into multiple corporations. Because the subsidy was per corporation, this legal fiction increased the subsidies. Courts looked through this sham and Obamacare specifically forbids this strategy.

These rules avoid games such as a restaurant setting up one corporation for servers, one for cooks, and so on, to have each "separate" corporation have fewer than 50 employees. Most reasonable people would agree that such a strategy is an abuse of the corporate form. However, the rules provide a trap for the unwary business owner who has more than one business or has set up multiple corporations for other reasons. If you own more than one business, you need to get advice on how the rules affect your situation.

C. HOW TO COUNT TO 50 EMPLOYEES

Let's shift our attention to the number of employees. The employer mandate basically says (1) if an organization has 50 or more full-time or full-time equivalent employees, (2) then it must offer government approved insurance to its full-time employees. The penalty applies only if a full-time employee is not offered insurance and then receives a subsidy for an exchange-based policy. In other words, the employer might fail to offer insurance to its full-time employees but if no employee obtains a subsidy there is no penalty on the employer.

Because the employer cannot control what its employees do, for planning purposes we assume that if the employer does not offer compliant insurance an employee will trigger the ShaRP by buying insurance on an exchange and obtaining a credit. We also caution against assuming that a highly paid employee will not qualify for a subsidy, because it is possible that an employee or even a spouse might have investment losses lowering income enough to qualify for a subsidy. Again, note that the employer cannot discriminate or retaliate against an employee who buys an exchange policy.

In February 2013, the IRS issued a 145 page proposed set of regulations as to how to determine whether an employer has 50 employees. As of this writing, the regulations are not final but the proposals at least provide some guidance as to where the rules will likely end up. Next, we examine these proposed rules.

1. THE BASICS—EASY SITUATIONS

To be full-time, a worker must average 30 or more hours per week. Keep in mind that in other contexts 40 hours per week is full-time, but not with Obamacare. We next have to compute how part-time workers count toward the 50 limit. A group of part-timers will count as full-time equivalent employees depending on the number of hours worked. For example, two half-time workers (15 hours/week) count as one full-time worker when figuring out whether the company has gone over 50. Here is a more detailed example:

Workers	24
Hours/Month	80 per worker
Total Hours/Month	1920
(Total Hours/Month) / 120 = Full-Time Equivalent Employees	
1920 / 120 = 16	

So in this case, our 24 part-time employees count as 16 full-time employees.

2. SALARIED EMPLOYEES

For salaried workers, we have to figure out how to count hours to determine if the salaried worker is full-time. In its guidance to date, the IRS has proposed three methods.
 (1) Tracking actual hours worked.
 (2) Tracking days worked and assuming the salaried worker worked 8 hours each day.
 (3) Tracking weeks worked and assuming the salaried worker worked 40 hours each week.

The employer can use different methods for different classes of employees, but must be consistent within each class. In addition, the employer cannot use an estimated method if it substantially understates the actual hours worked. For example, if a salaried worker worked three 12-hour days each week for a total of 36 hours and thus full-time status, it would likely be improper to use the "tracking days" method to lower that to a total of 24 hours by counting three 8-hour days. Again, this is not the final rule so if you have salaried employees, you will have to check the final rule when it comes out.

If a company has a stable workforce with steady hours throughout the year, this calculation is not too bad. For companies with workforces that vary throughout the year or with a lot of turnover, the calculations become extremely difficult.

The first step here for the employer is to make as clear as possible which employees are full-time and which are part-time. If possible, keep part-time workers below 30 hours per week, every week. Some companies are already limiting workers to 28 or 29 hours per week. An employee who never works over 30 hours per week can never average more than 30 hours per week. Another important step will be to keep excellent records of each employee's hours worked, including salaried employees.

3. SEASONAL WORKERS

Nonetheless, many businesses are seasonal and the law attempts to accommodate this reality. What if a company balloons up over 50 employees for short periods of time, like retailers over the holidays or farms during harvest? These cases provide one of the toughest challenges in how to count to 50.

The Obamacare statute provides that if a company goes over 50 due to hiring seasonal workers, it is not a large employer so long as the number of full-time employees exceeds 50 for less than 120 days. So what's a "seasonal worker?"

Seasonal workers include (1) retail workers at the holidays and (2) those defined in CFR 500.20(s)(1) as seasonal workers. CFR 500.20(s)(1) defines "seasonal workers" as workers whose employment pertains to (1) work that is done only at particular times of the year and (2) which by its nature cannot be done throughout the year, such as much agricultural work. However, the next section, CFR 500.20(s)(2), defines "temporary workers" as those who work on a particular piece of work for a short time. By implication Obamacare does not count that kind of temporary worker as seasonal. It appears that we can be fairly certain holiday retail workers and many agricultural workers are "seasonal," but other industries are still up in the air at this point. The employer bears the burden of proving it qualifies for this seasonal worker exemption, increasing the employer's risk.

3. TEMPORARY WORKERS AND INDEPENDENT CONTRACTORS

A particularly thorny problem for many companies will be how to deal with temporary workers and certain kinds of independent contractors (sometimes called "leased workers"). Can an organization avoid counting and offering insurance to temps who are paid through an agency? Can an organization avoid counting workers who are independent contractors?

The IRS has signaled it will be very aggressive in how it treats temps. Obamacare and the IRS look to the definition of a "common law employee" in determining what is required. According to the IRS, "[u]nder common-law rules, anyone who performs services for you is your employee *if you can control what will be done and how it will be done.* This is so even when you give the employee freedom of action. What matters is that you have the right to control the details of how the services are performed" (emphasis in the original). Although there is no hard and fast rule, the three factors considered are (1) degree of control the employer has; (2) the financial arrangements with the worker; and (3) the type of relationship between the employer and worker.

Many temporary workers and independent contractors could fall within the definition of a common law employee, meaning they count toward the 50 threshold and that a large employer would have to offer insurance if they work enough hours. Why should you care? Failing to offer affordable insurance to temps could trigger the ShaRP based on all your employees under the Big Risk Rule, not just the temps. If the

IRS re-categorized temps as full-time employees and caused a large employer to fall below the 95% offer threshold, the penalty would be (Number of Employees – 30) * $2000. You will need to work closely with any temp agency you use to make sure everyone is in compliance and who is responsible if you are not.

We would add one other point. If an agency provides a temporary worker who works over 30 hours per week, does the agency have to offer insurance? At the time of writing, we have not seen definitive guidance. There has been some discussion that such a worker could count as a full-time employee for both the temp agency and the organization where the temp works. From the IRS's perspective, being able to collect the penalty twice would be a good thing. Once again, work closely with your advisors to determine how the final rules apply to your situation.

4. FOREIGN-BASED WORKERS

Another detail is whether full-time employees working overseas count toward the 50 limit. The IRS has issued guidance stating that they will not. If your organization employs workers in foreign countries, you will need to check what the final rule says. In addition, it appears that a large foreign company with a small U.S. presence with fewer than 50 U.S.-based employees would count as small.

5. CONCLUSION AND IMPORTANT STEPS TO TAKE

Some management steps seem clear. Each employer must keep excellent records of how much each employee works, including salaried workers. In addition, the status of each employee must be kept as clear as possible. Using seasonal and temporary workers will require a great deal of planning to avoid running afoul of the rules. Lastly, each employer will have to gauge competitive factors to determine whether an offer of health insurance makes sense for the organization.

D. COMPLIANT POLICY—MINIMUM VALUE AND AFFORDABILITY

At this point, whether a business has a compliant health insurance plan bears the most uncertainty. To comply, the policy must cover at least 60% of the expected cost of benefits paid. For example, if it is statistically expected that there will be $100,000 in benefits paid during the year, the plan and the employer must be expected to pay at least $60,000 and the employees no more than $40,000.

For a pool of employees, this calculation becomes impossible for anyone other than professional actuaries. The IRS plans to put up a website where an employer can input data for the company and find out if the policy complies. If the plan meets the tests in the IRS website for affordability, it should be considered affordable.

What happens if a company fails to check affordability and offers insurance that turns out not to be affordable? Here is one of the biggest risks—a company could buy insurance but not be in compliance. The company could incur the expense of insurance AND still be subject to the Obamacare ShaRP if it does not pass the minimum value test. In that situation, there is also a chance that the employees, even though they have insurance, might not have good enough insurance to meet the individual mandate and could end up paying the personal penalty tax.

Next, we have to test the policy for affordability to each employee. If the employee's required contribution exceeds 9.5% of the employee's household income the policy will be considered unaffordable. If the employee receives a subsidy to buy an exchange-based policy, the employer will be liable for the ShaRP.

The IRS has recognized that employers do not normally have access to an employee's investment income information or spouse's income information and therefore has no way of knowing the employee's family income. What happens if the offer calls for less than 9.5% of the employee's W2 income but the employee's family has losses making the offer cost more than 9.5% of family income? Employers normally do not have access to this personal information on every employee.

To solve this problem, the IRS has offered a safe harbor based on the employee's W2 income, the income figure the employer does know. Other safe harbors have also been proposed and you should check with your advisors about the final rules to see if one is both approved and helpful to your organization.

E. AUTOMATIC ENROLLMENT AND 90-DAY LIMIT ON WAITING PERIODS

For companies with over 200 full-time employees, Obamacare requires that all employees be automatically enrolled in the company's health plan when hired. The employee can opt out if the employee chooses. However, the government says it will be ready in 2014 to implement the automatic enrollment rules, but as of the time of writing the regulations remain unwritten. If your organization has over 200 full-time employees, you will have to determine when the automatic enrollment rules apply.

F. WHO MUST RECEIVE AN OFFER OF INSURANCE AND WHEN?

Which employees must receive offers of insurance? We know the answer is full-time employees but determining full-time status can be difficult in particular situations. The IRS has provided some proposed guidance setting forth three categories of employees. The rules differ for each kind of employee.

1. FULL-TIME EMPLOYEES AND DEPENDENTS (30 HOURS/WEEK OR MORE)

First, a person reasonably expected to be full-time for a year must receive an offer of insurance within 90 days of hire. Of course, a company could offer insurance sooner if it chooses. Keep in mind that a temp or independent contractor might count as a common law worker and be entitled to an insurance offer. The IRS has the power to assess a penalty of $100 per day per employee for violation of the 90-day rule. Employers face great risk for failing to offer in a timely fashion or misclassifying a worker.

Obamacare forbids one obvious scheme: disband the corporation and immediately reincorporate to "erase" the history of ongoing employees. An unscrupulous employer might reason that because a new employee need not be offered insurance until after 90 days, the solution is to just reincorporate every 90 days to make everyone "new" repeatedly. The law forbids this strategy.

Obamacare requires large employers to offer health insurance to full-time employees and dependents. As of this writing, the IRS has issued guidance stating that the employer must offer insurance to (1) the employee and (2) dependent children up to the age of 26, but (3) not to spouses of employees. "Child" includes natural and adopted children, stepchildren, and "eligible foster children" of the employee. A plan may, but not must, offer coverage to dependents other than a child of the employee such as a grandchild, niece or nephew as well as spouses.

2. PART-TIME EMPLOYEES (LESS THAN 30 HOURS/WEEK)

Let's move to part-time employees. If a person is part-time and will be kept under 30 hours per week, the company need not offer insurance. The average will always be under 30 if the employee never works more than 30 hours per week.

3. VARIABLE HOUR AND SEASONAL EMPLOYEES (WHERE WE ARE NOT SURE)

Now it gets harder. A variable hour employee is an employee where it is not clear if he or she will be full-time for a year or not. For example, a company might hire someone for 40 hours per week over the holidays with the intent of cutting back the hours after the rush season. The annual average would then fall below 30 hours per week.

For such workers whose hours may vary and sometimes go over 30 hours per week, the IRS has proposed a rule where we essentially wait and see how much the employee actually works. The employer defines an initial measurement period, standard measurement period, and stability period for itself. We explain what exactly those terms mean below.

This gets extremely technical. If the employee averages over 30 hours during the initial measurement period, the company must offer insurance over the next period (the stability period). We then re-compute the employee's average hours over the next measurement period (standard measurement period) and offer insurance in the next stability period if the average exceeds 30 hours per week.[8] Examples will help clarify the rule.

One example the IRS gives is for a large employer with more than 50 full-time employees. On December 1, the employer hires a new employee with the intent that the employee will be a permanent full-time worker. The employer must offer the employee insurance by March or pay a penalty. There is no penalty during the 90-day waiting period in December, January or February.

A second example the IRS gives is a seasonal worker. In December, January and February the employee works 35 hours per week, which by itself would be full-time. However, In March, April and May the employee only works 20 hours per week. If the facts and circumstances indicate the first three months were a busy season and the intent was for the employee to go to part-time later, this seasonal worker does not count toward 50 employees and there is no requirement to offer insurance.

What are the rules for the various periods that the employer must set for itself? Under the proposed guidance, the initial measurement period (i.e. the time we measure a new variable hour employee) can be

---

8   The IRS is considering a rule that would allow for an administra-
     tive period between the standard measurement period and the stabil-
     ity period. Basically, the idea is to allow time to compute whether the
     employee worked enough in the standard measurement period to be
     entitled to an insurance offer in the subsequent stability period.

from 3 to 12 months. The standard measurement period (i.e. the time we measure ongoing employees to determine whether they qualify as full-time for the next period) similarly must be 3 to 12 months. The stability period (i.e. the time the employer must offer insurance to employees working enough hours to count as full-time) has to be at least 6 months but cannot be shorter than the initial measurement period or standard measurement period.

Here is a chart with some examples:

Initial Measurement Period	Standard Measurement Period	Stability Period
3 Months	3 Months	6 Months
6 Months	6 Months	6 to 12 Months
12 Months	12 Months	12 Months

Suppose a variable hour employee averages less than 30 hours per week in the initial period. We then re-measure in the next period, called the standard measurement period. If such an ongoing employee exceeds 30 hours per week in this next period, then the employee is entitled to an insurance offer in the next stability period. That is true even if the employee will be less than 30 hours per week in the subsequent period. The employee's insurance offer applies to the entire stability period.

The IRS guidance requires a second test. Even if the variable hour employee is part-time under these period measurement rules, we must look at the average for the entire calendar year as well. If the employee is full-time in a calendar year, that employee is entitled to an offer of insurance.

At this time, no guidance has been provided regarding a part-time employee who is offered full-time employment. It seems logical that the 90-day rule for new employees would apply, but that is unknown at this time. Even if we apply the 90-day rule, do we count from the original employment date or from the start of full-time status? The safest approach may be to offer insurance right away in that case. Hopefully, the IRS will issue specific guidance in the near future. In addition, we have found no indication of how to measure the hours of an employee who misses work for an extended period due to injury or illness.

It will depend on the employer's situation and preferences for determining whether having long or short initial measurement periods and standard measurement periods is better. There is a tradeoff: a longer measurement period will smooth out short-term spikes in the average hours worked and increase the amount of time before an offer is necessary. However, the longer measurement periods require longer stability periods. Variable hour employees qualifying as full-time will be entitled to a longer period of insurance. Competitive factors, employee turnover and retention issues will drive this decision.

REFERENCES AND FURTHER READING

For a good review of the employer mandate in a Q&A format, go to http://www.piperreport.com/blog/2013/01/02/employer-mandate-afford-able-care-act-irs-answers-questions-aca-employer-mandate/.

For a discussion of the recent proposed regulations on "how to count to 50" as well as details on enforcement, go to http://www.martindale.com/health-care-law/article_Holland-Hart-LLP_1692200.htm.

For a good overview of the limits on gamesmanship in "counting to 50" under Obamacare, go to http://www.balch.com/files/Publication/ce075aac-8a2c-436e-8eff-12316eca2f53/Presentation/PublicationAttachment/e1a6e06c-5532-4359-a92b-1a6417bcde22/Let's%20Get%20Small_Newsletter_July12.pdf.

For some novel and aggressive compliance strategies, go to http://www.paulhastings.com/assets/publications/2328.pdf.

For a breakdown of the guidance on seasonal workers, go to http://www.towerswatson.com/en-US/Insights/Newsletters/Americas/health-care-reform-bulletin/2012/guidance-arrives-on-safe-harbor-methods-to-determine-full-time-employee-status.

For an excellent discussion of the proposed rules regarding variable hour and part time employees, go to http://www.towerswatson.com/en-US/Insights/Newsletters/Americas/health-care-reform-bulletin/2012/guidance-arrives-on-safe-harbor-methods-to-determine-full-time-employee-status.

For information regarding foreign companies and foreign employees, a good starting point is http://www.mondaq.com/unitedstates/x/231818/employee+rights+labour+relations/US+Healthcare+Reform+Foreign+Employers+And+Employers+Of+Foreign+Workers.

For the recent guidance regarding salaried workers and other rules regarding classifying workers as full or part-time, go to http://www.lexology.com/library/detail.aspx?g=a06dedef-00b9-4b67-9827-d8da81f394a5.

For details on how the IRS views temporary workers and defines common law employees, go to http://www.irs.gov/Businesses/Small-Businesses-&-Self-Employed/Independent-Contractor-(Self-Employed)-or-Employee%3F.

A good starting point for investigating what "minimum essential benefits" is going to mean is here http://ebn.benefitnews.com/news/hhs-defines-essential-health-benefits-ppaca-2729494-1.html.

For suggested best practices regarding variable employees, go to
http://www.crawfordadvisors.com/employee-benefits-news/
ppaca-tips-best-practices-penalties-variable-employees.

For a brief discussion of some of the employer actions that could trigger the $100 per
day per employee fine, see http://www.the-alliance.org/uploadedFiles/Members/
Learning_Circles/In_the_Circle/2010_08Aug18_ALC%20Exec%20Summary.pdf.

For a good discussion of the proposed W-2 income safe harbor, as well
as other proposed safe harbors, see http://www.shrm.org/legalis-
sues/federalresources/pages/affordability-safe-harbors.aspx.

For a discussion of the delay of implementation of auto-enrollment, go
to http://www.seyfarth.com/publications/MA022112.

For further further examples of the calculation of the employer mandate penalty in various situations, go to http://www.nfib.com/
Portals/0/PDF/AllUsers/Free%20Rider%20Provision.pdf.

CHAPTER 10:

TRANSITION RULES

What You Will Need

✦ *Dates for current plans*
✦ *Enrollment periods for current plans*
✦ *Plan that was in place on December 27, 2012*

Many health plans do not operate on a calendar year. Suppose a plan starts July 1, 2013 and ends June 30, 2014. Must it comply with Obamacare?[9]

Under current guidance, Obamacare's mandates will not apply until the first day of its new fiscal year in 2014 if (1) the employer offered coverage under any such plan as of December 27, 2012, and (2) at least one third of the employer's full-time employees were eligible for coverage and at least one fourth of them actually participated. If the large employer does not meet this safe harbor, it will need to

---

9   The government recently announced delay of enforcement of the employer mandate to 2015. It is unclear what effect that delay has on the transition rules written before the delay.

get a new plan going into 2014 that meets Obamacare's mandates to avoid the ShaRP.

A strategy some are pursuing is to change their plan to run from December 1 to December 1, or some other dates late in the year. This allows a plan beginning December 1, 2013 to run through December 1, 2014 to escape many of the Obamacare mandates for almost a year (provided it meets the safe harbor requirements). By December 2014, it may be much more clear what the sensible course of action is than in late 2013 or early 2014.

Another transition rule deals with computing whether a company is a large employer with 50 or more full-time employees. At the time of this writing, the IRS is planning to allow employers to use any six-month period in 2013 to count employees to determine whether it is large in 2014. If you are just over 50 full-time employees now and want to be "small" in 2014 you need to act quickly. What you do now could greatly impact your available options next year.

REFERENCES AND FURTHER READING

For a discussion of the proposed transition rules, go to http://www.crawfordadvi-sors.com/employee-benefits-news/irs_ppaca_new_er_mandate_guidance.

CHAPTER 11

GRANDFATHER CLAUSE

What You Will Need

✦ *Plan in effect on March 23, 2010*
✦ *Analysis of whether Obamacare compliant plan is better than the grandfathered plan*

Obamacare allows employers to keep an old plan and continue with it. This is known as the grandfather clause rule. Faced with the complexities of Obamacare, many organizations might want to just keep doing what they have been doing. Obamacare Sec. 1251 allows a plan to have grandfathered status, but this is a bit misleading. Even a grandfathered plan must comply with Obamacare in many ways. Although the rules are still being finalized, here is a summary of what we know at this time.

The critical date is March 23, 2010, the date of Obamacare's enactment. Only a plan in effect on that date even has the potential for grandfathered status.

No organization wants a plan set in stone forever. Here is what can change without losing grandfathered status.

1. New family members may enroll in established healthcare plans, as long as the plan allowed for such additions before March 23, 2010.

2. New employees may enroll in already established plans, as long as the policy allowed for such additions before March 23, 2010.

3. The insurer may terminate the healthcare plan if it gives advance notice but may not do so for health or medical reasons.

4. The insurer may change its premiums.

5. The plan can change to conform to Obamacare's requirements. That is, the plan can add provisions to provide required minimum essential benefits, for example.

Some provisions cannot change. If the plan changes in any of the following ways, it loses grandfathered status. If it fails to meet any Obamacare requirement, both the employer and employees will be subject to the penalties—both the annual per employee penalties as well as the $100 per employee per day penalties.

1. The elimination of all, or substantially all, benefits to treat a particular condition. Early indications are that the government will take an aggressive view of what counts as an elimination of benefits and provides a genuine trap for unwary business owners. If, for example, a psychologist treats a patient with medication and therapy, and the insurer eliminates therapy from coverage, then it is considered to have eliminated substantially all benefits to treat that condition. Over time, the coverages in grandfathered policies will likely become antiquated as medical technology advances. Also, an employer would need to be extremely vigilant to catch such a change if the insurer made it.

2. Any "significant" increase in the amount employees pay as their share. "Significant" means an increase of 15 percent plus medical inflation measured by the Consumer Price Index for All Urban Consumers, published by the Department of Labor.

3. Any decrease in the contribution rate by the employer or employee-based organization (like a union). For example, if the employer pays 80% and costs rise, the employer must pay at least 80% of the increased amount. Even a decrease in respect to family coverage, even though the contribution rate for self-only coverage remains the same, still results in the loss of grandfathered status.

4. Any forming of a new contract, policy, or certification will result in a loss of grandfathered status, after March 23, 2010.

5. Any change in insurance companies after March 23, 2010. We believe this provision could put great upward pressure on rates as the insurer would face no direct competition for the grandfathered plan, only indirect competition from new Obamacare-approved policies.

6. Any reduction in benefits due to changes in annual or lifetime limits.

Obamacare does not just leave grandfathered policies alone. As of 2011, all grandfathered policies are subject to the following rules and regulations of the Obamacare:

1. All group healthcare plan providers must submit a written statement to their employees and HHS, declaring that they believe their plan qualifies as a grandfathered policy per Sec. 1251 of Obamacare.

2. All group healthcare plan providers must provide employees with contact information to HHS to file complaints and ask questions.

3. All grandfathered plans may not impose any preexisting condition exclusions and shall not require any waiting period exceeding 90 days.

4. Group health plans may not establish lifetime limits on the dollar value of benefits for any participant or beneficiary. For plans taking effect prior to January 1, 2014, any annual limits must be "essential" to health benefits. It is not entirely clear what this means so we urge caution in relying on this provision.

5. The anti-rescission rule applies to grandfathered policies, forbidding insurers from rescinding policies absent fraud or intentional misrepresentation. Traditionally, insurers could rescind (i.e. retroactively cancel) a policy for misstatements of material fact in an insurance application, whether those misstatements were intentional or not.

6. A group health plan must cover dependents until the age of 26 years.

7. The plan must provide uniform explanation of coverage documents and standardized definitions, as laid forth by the National Association of Insurance Commissioners (NAIC), to enrollees and the HHS.

The bottom line is that keeping a grandfathered policy will be difficult to do. Even a small mistake could subject the employer to exposure to the ShaRP. The employer could purchase insurance yet still pay a fine for failing to buy the "right" insurance. In addition, employees would not be able to prove they have proper coverage and would have to pay the penalty tax as well. Not a good day at the office when that happens. In addition, the employer will have little leverage with its insurer which will likely force premiums up. For most cases, the grandfathered plan would have to have huge advantages to offset the downside risk.

Even more troubling, factors beyond the employer's control could impact grandfathered status. An employee organization, like a union providing group healthcare coverage, could violate Obamacare's grandfather rules but the employer would pay the fine. Similarly, the insurer could also make a change that the employer did not notice in time.

Moreover, if an insurance company went through a merger or buyout, would the plan still be grandfathered? In either case, the contracts, policies, or companies could change. No one really knows what would happen in those cases.

REFERENCES AND FURTHER READING

The Department of Labor's guidance regarding grandfathered plans
is here http://www.dol.gov/ebsa/faqs/faq-aca2.html.

For a detailed discussion of the grandfather clause rules, go to
http://www.groom.com/media/publication/728_GLG%20
Grandfather%20Rule%20-%206-15-10%20final.pdf.

CHAPTER 12:

SELF-FUNDING PLANS

What You Will Need

✦ *Risk assessment of employee pool*
✦ *Comparison of insured plan vs. self-funding plan*

Obamacare leaves open the possibility of a company having a self-funding plan, sometimes called a self-insured plan. Self-funding plans enjoy many exemptions from Obamacare and therefore are potentially much less expensive. Traditionally, self-funding plans have been solely for very large companies, but now companies as small as 25 employees are using them.

A self-funding plan typically works as follows. The employer pays into a trust fund over time from employer and employee contributions. Medical claims are paid from that fund as they arise. The employer hires a plan administrator to administer the claims. To deal with the risk that a large claim might exceed the fund, the employer buys a stop-loss insurance policy covering claims beyond a set amount (called the deductible). Basically, the employer pays for small items and the stop-loss policy covers major losses.

Here are some of the potential advantages of a self-funding plan:

(1) Self-funding plans are less regulated under Obamacare and are exempt from its taxes on insurance policies.

(2) There is no need to participate in the risk-adjustment system, which essentially requires insurers with lots of healthy participants to pay into a fund for insurers with less healthy participants. An organization with a healthy pool of employees would end up paying less than it would under Obamacare.

(3) Medical loss ratio and premium increase rules do not apply. Because the insurance company has more freedom, in theory it may be able to charge lower premiums.

(4) Because the plans are governed by ERISA, state mandates and premium taxes do not apply to self-funding plans. For companies with employees in multiple states, this allows uniform benefits company-wide. The downside is that ERISA is extremely complex in its own right and a self-funding plan would need to comply with it.

(5) Potential cost savings that might be enough to avoid the Cadillac plan tax (see Chapter 14) in 2018.

As with most things in life, there are catches:

(1) No guaranteed issue. Unlike a plan under Obamacare, the stop-loss insurer can decline to issue a policy if the employee pool looks too risky.

(2) No guaranteed renewal. Unlike a plan under Obamacare, the stop-loss insurer can decline to renew a policy.

(3) No all-comers rule. Unlike a plan under Obamacare, the stop-loss insurer can exclude high-risk individuals from coverage.

(4) Less regulation. The stop-loss insurer enjoys much greater freedom from state and federal regulation, sometimes to the detriment of the employer or employees.

Self-funding plans are not a free-for-all. Despite the relative freedom compared to Obamacare compliant plans, self-funding plans are still subject to many regulations, too numerous to list here. Self-funding plans must still offer minimum essential benefits. Self-funding plans are subject to HIPAA, ERISA, COBRA, federal anti-discrimination laws, and any number of other regulations.

Self-funding plans probably make the most sense for companies with young, healthy workforces. Such a risk pool is attractive to the stop-loss insurer. What makes these plans cheaper also makes them unavailable to some employers. The bottom line is that the self-funding plan could be a good option. You should check with your insurance advisors to find out if they make sense for your company.

REFERENCES AND FURTHER READING

For a discussion of how Obamacare affects self-funding plans, go to
http://www.cpbjnow.com/article/20130104/HEALTHCARE/120929731/-1/
health-care-reform&template=HCR.

For a news article about the possibility of even small companies using self-funding
plans, go to http://www.usatoday.com/story/money/business/2013/03/14/
some-small-businesses-choose-to-self-insure/1988481/.

CHAPTER 13:

SMALL BUSINESS TAX CREDITS

What You Will Need

✦ *Number of employees, Average wage per employee, Amount spent on health insurance*

The law provides a tax credit for small businesses and even small tax-exempt employers to encourage them to provide health insurance. These credits are available even if a company has losses, unlike the benefits of a deduction. For 2010-2013, a qualifying business gets up to a 35% credit and a tax-exempt organization up to 25%. In 2014, the credit increases to 50% and 35% respectively. The law does not provide for credits beyond 2014.

To qualify, the business must have:

(1) Fewer than 25 full-time or full-time equivalent employees;

(2) An average wage of less than $50,000 per year.

The IRS provides some examples. First, we look at an auto mechanic shop and compute the credits for both 2013 and 2014.

```
Employees                    10
Total Wages                  $250,000
Average Wage                 $250,000/10 = $25,000
Healthcare Costs             $70,000
2013 Credit = 35% * $70,000 = $24,500
2014 Credit = 50% * $70,000 = $35,000
```

Another IRS example uses a small non-profit entity. Again, we compute the credit for both 2013 and 2014.

```
Employees                    9
Total Wages                  $198,000
Average Wage                 $198,000/9 = $22,000
Healthcare Costs             $72,000
2013 Credit = 25% * $72,000 = $18,000
2014 Credit = 35% * $72,000 = $25,200
```

For a small organization, the tax credit might very well be worth pursuing. If you are a small employer with a workforce with modest wages, contact your tax advisor as the credit could be worth a lot to your organization. For more details, see IRS Form 8941. However, where these calculations become tricky is where there is a lot of turnover or seasonal workers. You will likely need a tax professional to help you in those situations.

REFERENCES AND FURTHER READING

For details on Obamacare's small business tax credit, go to http://www.irs.gov/uac/Small-Business-Health-Care-Tax-Credit-for-Small-Employers.

CHAPTER 14:

NEW TAXES

What You Will Need

✦ *How much does your plan cost per employee, especially going forward?*

✦ *Do I run a tanning salon?*

✦ *Do I make or import medical devices?*

Obamacare introduces a number of new taxes. We highlight a few of them here. See your tax advisor for a detailed analysis of your situation.

A. CADILLAC PLAN TAX

Not only does Obamacare penalize large employers too miserly to pay for coverage, it punishes those who are too generous. In 2018, if the value of health benefits exceeds $10,200 for an individual or $27,500 for a family, there is a steep tax of 40% on the excess.

Here are examples:

```
Single Employee
    $12,000 value of plan
    Tax = ($12,000 - $10,200) * 40% = $720
```

```
Family of Four Example
    $33,500 value of plan
    Tax = ($33,500 - $27,500) * 40% = $2400
```

This Cadillac plan tax will most likely hit union companies, municipalities, and state entities like universities most severely. Organizations currently negotiating long-term collective bargaining agreements need to consider the impact of this tax now even though it does not apply until 2018. We also note that there is a formula for adjusting the initial thresholds of $10,200 and $27,500 if health costs rise more quickly than anticipated. In other words, the law seeks to avoid having too many plans subject to the tax if premiums rise more than expected. In addition, the threshold can be adjusted for employers with employees aged 55-64 as well as employees in high-risk jobs. Those situations put upward pressure on premiums but the law seeks to avoid imposing the Cadillac tax on organizations with an older workforce.

B. TANNING TAX

If you run a tanning salon, you are already subject to a tax on tanning. The tax of 10% of revenues has been in effect since 2010.

C. MEDICAL DEVICE TAX

Obamacare imposes a 2.3% tax on the manufacture or import of medical devices, effective 2013. "Medical device" is defined in Sec. 201(h) of the Federal Food, Drug and Cosmetic Act as any instrument, apparatus, implement, machine, contrivance, implant, in vitro reagent, or other similar article, including any component, part or accessory that is intended for use in diagnosis or treatment of a human disease or is intended to affect the structure or function of the body. Medical device does not include drugs. Check with your tax advisor if you believe your product potentially falls in this category.

There is a retail exemption in the statute and proposed rules. Some products sold at retail are exempt from the tax. The statute specifically exempts eyeglasses, contact lenses, hearing aids, and any other device HHS determines "to be of the type that is generally purchased by the general public at retail for personal use." However, the government is still writing rules for other specific products.

At this time, the IRS proposes a "facts and circumstances" test for determining whether products like custom orthotics, orthodontics, dental crowns and fillings are exempt or not. The IRS has provided some proposed guidance, suggesting that if consumers who are not medical professionals can purchase the device directly and safely use the product with little or no training it probably falls within the retail exemption. The IRS is also considering a safe harbor for devices defined as "over the counter" by the FDA or devices that count as "durable medical equipment" within the meaning of 42 CFR 414.202.

"Facts and circumstances" is what lawyers say when they mean "we'll know it when we see it." Unfortunately, there is no clear guidance yet for these other industries and if this tax potentially affects your business, we can only direct you to your tax advisors.

REFERENCES AND FURTHER READING

For more details on the Cadillac plan tax, go to http://www. cigna.com/aboutus/health-care-reform/faqs.

The IRS has a list of Obamacare taxes here, including the tanning tax http://www.irs.gov/uac/Affordable-Care-Act-Tax-Provisions.

For further information on the medical device tax as well as a link to the proposed guidance, go to http://www.jwterrill.com/wp/?p=1851.

CHAPTER 15:

WELLNESS

What You Will Need

✦ *Analysis of whether a wellness plan makes sense for your organization*

Obamacare encourages employers to adopt wellness programs. The rules are still being finalized, but the basic idea is that employers provide financial rewards for employees to do things like lose weight, lower cholesterol, or quit smoking. The government sets limits on the size of the rewards and punishments, with exceptions for people who cannot or should not try to reach the goals. An ounce of prevention is worth a pound of cure, wellness advocates would argue.

Employers will have to decide whether such programs are worth the expense. In addition, many commentators fear lawsuits against employers for discrimination and invasion of privacy. The obvious risk is that the incentives lead to preferring employees who are younger, healthier and weigh less getting paid more, to the detriment of the old, disabled or heavy, all potentially protected classes under state or federal discrimination laws. Should employers have access to detailed health information on each employee? What if the information is misused or there is a security breach? Some employers may simply believe regulating employee conduct in this way is not their job. Check with your insurance provider and legal advisors to see if this kind of program makes sense for your organization.

REFERENCES AND FURTHER READING

For further information regarding the wellness rules and available options, go to http://www.healthleadersmedia.com/page-1/HEP-286769/ PPACA-Rules-on-Wellness-Programs-Could-Push-Participation.

A collection of links to various guidance on wellness is here http://www.lifehealth-pro.com/2012/12/03/ppaca-rate-wellness-and-benefits-proposals-roll-o.

Another article on wellness rules http://rss.ubabenefits.com/tabid/2835/Default. aspx?art=PDX%2FgnXBLPo%3D&mfid=XecEv5Wrckw%3D.

CHAPTER 16:

STRATEGY CONSIDERATIONS

What You Will Need

- *Assess importance of insurance to employee recruitment and retention*
- *Analysis of competitiveness*
- *Integration of human resource and insurance strategy with the overall business strategy*
- *Consideration of administrative and information technology needs for each available option*
- *Consideration of the ethical implications of your decision*

A. SHOULD WE OFFER HEALTH INSURANCE?

This is where the rubber hits the road. In the next few chapters, we set out the main options available to business owners and other employers.

First, we will cover some of the general business considerations that could help guide your decisions. Next, we will break down the available options by the size of company.

All employers, regardless of size, will have to consider just how important health insurance coverage is for employee recruiting and retention. Ask yourself whether you would lose current employees or have trouble attracting talent in the future if you failed to offer good health insurance. Is retention of employees important because of steep learning curves and high training costs? For those of you in unionized industries, how important is the health plan to the union? We encourage all employers to seriously analyze exactly why (or even why not) they offer health insurance. Lawyers and accountants tend to focus on the rules, you as the employer need to think about the business considerations.

Human resource strategy needs to be part of your overall business strategy. Some businesses need top-flight benefits packages to attract and retain talent. If your best talent joins your competitors, your organization will lose. In that situation, the company's strategy necessarily requires doing whatever is possible to attract good employees. In other industries, however, benefits are less important. Keeping costs down might be more important to remaining competitive. You will have to analyze what is best for your organization.

B. MANAGING CHANGE

Whatever your organization does with regard to healthcare, odds are that Obamacare will require changes. Change can sometimes be threatening to people, especially when that change affects the basic need of healthcare. Management will need to think carefully about how to manage the reactions of employees to any changes that are forthcoming to avoid damaging morale.

In addition, consider the resources required to implement your plan. Referring your employees to the exchanges requires little in the way of a human resources department or information technology support. Managing a self-funding plan can be difficult and time consuming. Staying on top of a grandfathered plan or even a plan through a broker will require some time and effort on the part of management. Make sure you consider every cost applicable to the solution you choose.

C. CHOOSING A PLAN

Many of the factors in choosing a plan will not change under Obamacare. For example, what physicians and hospitals are available in a network will still be important. How much of the cost the employees bear through premiums, co-pays and deductibles will still be critical. Of course, the total premium makes a big difference as well.

Obamacare alters this decision-making process, however. Most traditional plans tend to be one size fits all, or something close to it, for all the employees. Employees don't mind so much because most people have little alternative to their employer provided plan. With the exchanges, however, employees have a much greater deal of control for how much the plan will cost them. People who don't mind risk and paying out of pocket may be happy with a bronze plan; those who want the plan to pay for almost everything can choose gold or platinum. In addition, the employees will be able to select from plans with different networks and can pick the one they like. When choosing whether or not to offer coverage, consider whether you as the employer can make those decisions more wisely than your employees and whether they might be happier choosing their own plans—with a little raise to offset the increased cost.

D. SUMMARY OF MANDATE AND TAX CREDITS BY BUSINESS SIZE

	Very Small Employer	Small Employer	Large Employer
Number of Employees	Less than 25	25 to 49	50 or more
Minimum Essential Benefits	If an employer offers a policy, possible penalty of $100 per day per employee for failing to offer minimum essential benefits.	If an employer offers a policy, possible penalty of $100 per day per employee for failing to offer minimum essential benefits.	If an employer offers a policy, possible penalty of $100 per day per employee for failing to offer minimum essential benefit.
Employer Mandate to Offer Insurance	No.	No.	Yes. Failure to offer insurance could lead to penalty. (Number of Employees – 30) * $2000
Employer Mandate to Offer Affordable Insurance	No.	No.	Yes. Offer of unaffordable insurance could lead to penalty of $3000 per employee not offered affordable insurance.
Small Business Tax Credit	Yes. A very small employer that offers insurance may be eligible for a tax credit depending on the average salary of employees.	No.	No.

E. ETHICAL CONCERNS

Another factor to consider is whether it is right or wrong to offer health insurance coverage. Some employers believe that offering good health benefit plans is a way of helping their employees' families lead better lives. Others see health insurance as merely a cost of doing business. In addition, you need to consider how other stakeholders in your organization will perceive your decisions, especially if you decide to drop coverage. Will the stigma of being a "bad" company hurt that much? Will the halo effect you get from being a "good" company benefit the organization? Only you can answer those questions, but we urge you to at least ask them.

REFERENCES AND FURTHER READING

For information on coordinating HR strategy with the overall business strategy, go to http://www.forbes.com/sites/edwardlawler/2012/08/15/corporate-strategy-how-hr-can-become-a-player/.

For the traditional factors to consider when purchasing a health plan, go to http://www.healthplanone.com/buying-health-insurance.aspx.

For a discussion of ethical considerations in HR, go to http://www.scu.edu/ethics/practicing/focusareas/business/ethics-human-resources.html.

CHAPTER 17:

FEWER THAN 25 FULL-TIME EMPLOYEES

What You Will Need

✦ *Fewer than 25 full-time or full-time equivalent employees*

✦ *Find out the average salary for each worker*

The rules vary for different sizes of organizations. If a company has fewer than 25 full-time employees,[10] it has considerable flexibility under Obamacare. There is no fear under Obamacare of paying penalties for failing to offer affordable insurance. In addition, Obamacare creates options to purchase insurance and obtain a tax credit to help offset the cost. Let's outline each option.

---

10   In the next few chapters, we assume you have gone through the process detailed above to determine the number of full-time equivalent employees. We just use number of full-time employees for convenience.

Option 1: Cover through an insured plan. A small company could keep its policy and seek grandfathered protection or purchase a plan through a broker or from an insurer. In addition, as set forth above, a small company may be eligible for a substantial tax credit. Remember, to get the tax credit you will also have to compute the average salary for your workforce.

You could also consider covering some but not all full-time employees. For example, it might be possible not to offer coverage to full-time employees eligible for Medicare. Before doing that, check with your tax, legal and insurance advisors to make sure you do not violate state or federal discrimination laws.

There is also the risk that the plan you offer does not fully comply with Obamacare, exposing the company to the risk that the IRS will impose the $100 per day per employee penalty. Although with an approved plan that risk would seem to be low, that risk is still present.

Option 2: Small Business Health Programs Program (SHOP). Small companies will be able to purchase coverage for their employees through the exchanges. Although Obamacare calls for a system where employees can pick from a number of competing plans, the government has announced that only one plan will be available through SHOP through 2014, deferring full implementation to 2015 at the earliest. States will have the option of defining a small employer as any number up to 100, so you will need to check the limit in your state. To purchase a SHOP policy, you will need to go your state's exchange and set up the plan there.

Option 3: Self-funding plan. As set forth above, a new trend is for even small companies to adopt self-funding insurance plans. Check with your insurance broker to see if this could be a viable option for your company. The administrative costs might be prohibitive and it may be difficult to find a stop-loss insurer for a small group, but it is probably worth at least talking to an insurance broker about the possibility.

Option 4: Drop coverage, no penalty tax. A small company has the option to drop coverage with no penalty. Employees would have to obtain coverage through Medicaid or the exchanges, or pay the penalty tax. One way to make this option go down with employees would be to share some of the savings—give raises for less than a health insurance plan costs to help employees purchase exchange policies and pocket the difference.

Option	Pros	Cons
Cover Through Insured Plan	•Employees like •Tax credit may be available in 2013 and 2014	•Expensive •Grandfather rules and risk
Small Business Health Options Program (SHOP)	•Employees Like •Should comply with Obamacare minimum benefit and value rules •Tax credit may be available in 2013 and 2014	•Expensive •Exchange policy quality not yet known
Self-funding Plan	•Employees like •Might be cheaper than other policies	•Could be expensive •Company might not qualify •Fewer protections from insurer
Drop Coverage	•Saves money •Employees get customized coverage •Saves administrative costs •Employees eligible for exchange subsidies or Medicaid •No penalty	•Employees won't like •Competition for new hires •Retention of employees

CHAPTER 18:

25-50 FULL-TIME EMPLOYEES

What You Will Need

✦ *Between 25 and 50 full-time or full-time equivalent employees*

The rules change if a company grows beyond 25 employees but still has fewer than 50 employees. Below 50 full-time employees, the employer is not subject to the penalty for failing to offer insurance. However, once the business goes over 25 it is no longer able to obtain the small business tax credits.

Let's look at the available options.

Option 1: Cover with grandfathered policy or through brokerage or from insurer. A small company does not have to provide coverage, but it can if it so desires. As with a company under 25 employees, you need to watch the discrimination rules if you decide to offer insurance to some full-time employees and not all. In addition, the policy you offer will have to comply with Obamacare, at the risk of the $100 per employee per day fine.

Option 2: SHOP could be available as well. Each state will set its own rules for SHOP, including the maximum number of employees to qualify. Check with your local state exchange to determine if your company qualifies.

Option 3: Self-funding plan. Again, self-funding plans are becoming available even for small firms. You should explore this possibility with your insurance advisors. As a somewhat bigger organization, your chances of finding a stop-loss insurer will likely be better than that for a smaller company.

Option 4: Drop coverage, no penalty tax. Again, as long as the company remains below 50 full-time employees, there is no penalty tax for failing to offer insurance. Employees would have to find coverage on their own as they would be subject to the individual mandate. The downside is that this approach could hurt employee morale and recruitment efforts. In addition, if you are close to 50 full-time employees it may limit your organization's growth if you feel you cannot hire more employees.

Option	Pros	Cons
Cover Through Insured Plan	•Employees like	•Expensive •Grandfather rules and risk •No tax credit
Small Business Health Options Program (SHOP)	•Employees Like •Should comply with Obamacare minimum benefit and value rules	•Expensive •Exchange policy quality not yet known
Self-funding Plan	•Employees like •Might be cheaper than other policies	•Could be expensive •Company might not qualify •Fewer protections from insurer
Drop Coverage	•Saves money •Employees get customized coverage •Saves administrative costs •Employees eligible for exchange subsidies or Medicaid •No penalty	•Employees won't like •Competition for new hires •Retention of employees

CHAPTER 19:

50 OR MORE
FULL-TIME EMPLOYEES

What You Will Need

✦ *More than 50 full-time or full-time equivalent employees*

Once a company exceeds 50 full-time employees, the ShaRP applies. The employer's options become more constrained. SHOP will not be available any time soon. Failing to provide coverage becomes much more expensive as the penalties can become hefty.

Again, a company could consider covering some but not all full-time employees. That carries a good deal of risk of a discrimination problem and you must check with your advisors before employing such a strategy. Also, keep in mind the 95% rule—large employers must offer health insurance to at least 95% of their full-time employees. Falling below 95%, even by mistake, can lead to large penalties based on the size of the entire organization. Similarly, relying on independent contractors and temporary employees might work, but recall that strategy is risky as well. Check with your advisors for exact guidance.

Option 1: Buy insurance through a plan. You could buy a new, Obamacare compliant plan or try to rely on a grandfathered plan. Remember, the grandfather rules are complicated and risky. You will likely need either outside advisors or an in-house staff to make sure you remain in compliance with Obamacare with regard to every employee.

Option 2: Self-funding plan. Large employers should look long and hard at the possibility of self-funding a plan. Check with your insurance broker to see if you company could qualify. In the long run, many believe self-funding to be the most affordable option. Self-funding plans will require a good deal of administrative support.

Option 3: Drop coverage, pay penalty. If the large employer drops coverage, then it must pay the ShaRP based on the entire workforce if any employee buys subsidized coverage on the exchange. Given the cost of health insurance, which we don't know exactly but which we know will be high, paying the ShaRP may be the more cost effective alternative.

Option	Pros	Cons
Cover Through Insured Plan	•Employees like •Avoids penalty	•Expensive •Grandfather rules and risk
Self-funding Plan	•Employees like •Might be cheaper than other policies	•Could be expensive •Company might not qualify •Fewer protections from insurer
Drop Coverage	•Saves money •Employees get customized coverage •Saves administrative costs •Employees eligible for exchange subsidies or Medicaid	•Employees won't like •Competition for new hires •Retention of employees •Potentially heavy penalties

CHAPTER 20:

STRATEGIES FOR PARTICULAR SITUATIONS

A. THE 49ER STRATEGY

For companies close to the 50 full-time employee cutoff, it is critical to manage the size and composition of the workforce. This is doubly true for companies of around 50 employees that plan to not offer health insurance.

The Obamacare rules assume a static world, but people are already adapting to them. The ShaRP kicks in at 50 employees, so an obvious strategy is to stay under 50 employees. This so-called 49er strategy, therefore, seeks to keep the business under 50 employees. Ways to do this would be to limit the company's growth, mechanize rather than hire, outsource rather than hire, make extensive use of overtime, or do whatever it takes to avoid hiring the 50th employee. Cutting to part-time, assuming the same number of hours, does not help the employer here because of the full-time equivalent rule.

49er Quick Example: A company offers no health coverage and has 50 full-time employees. In 2014, it will be subject to an Obamacare penalty of $40,000. Cutting one position into two half-time positions does not help avoid the penalty, because the two half-timers count as one full-time. Easiest solution-fire someone and get the job done with 49 employees. There's no obligation to buy insurance and no penalty because the company is below 50.

B. THE 29ER STRATEGY

This is where the second part of the rule comes in. Even if the organization has more than 50 full-time employees, it need only offer health coverage to full-time employees. There is no penalty for failing to offer insurance to part-time employees. Many people on both sides of the Obamacare debate seem not to understand this point. So even a company that has more than 50 full-time employees can achieve savings by cutting people to less than 30 hours per week.

This 29er strategy works well for companies in industries where health benefits are not necessary for attracting workers. Fast food and big retail come to mind.

29er Quick Example: Company has 50 full-time employees but offers coverage only to 5 key employees. This will lead to a penalty based on the entire workforce ((50-30) * $2000 = $40,000). Solution: Cut the 45 uncovered workers to half time and hire 45 more half time workers, leaving us with 5 full-time and 90 half time workers. The company has complied with Obamacare, as it has offered coverage to its full-time workers. It does not have to offer coverage to the half time workers and there is no penalty for not doing so.

One strategy we have seen involves employers facilitating the ability of their employees to work two part time jobs. For example, a local fast food restaurant dropped its prohibition on its employees working for another restaurant. Because many companies are already cutting their full-time employees to half-time, this rule change helps such companies "share" employees. Of course, this is not good for the employees who now have a less stable schedule and face the prospect of being penalized if they do not buy their own health insurance.

Another chain restaurant in our area has expanded its hiring of full-time employees. Current employees, however, fear that the company is expanding its pool of trained employees so that it can cut them to part-time next year. If the company is not really pursuing such a policy, its employees need a pep talk. If the company really is planning to cut everyone to part-time next year, the employees probably need an even bigger pep talk. In any organization, morale counts.

We use extreme examples here for illustrative purposes. You will have to consider the competitive impacts on your business of such moves. However, if your organization is close to the cut-offs, hiring one more worker or misclassifying a worker can be extremely costly.

C. MEDICAIDER STRATEGY

That brings us to another group we'll call the Medicaiders. If Medicaid is free and even subsidized exchange coverage costs something, some people might be in a position where a raise or increase in hours makes them ineligible for Medicaid but does not make up the cost of the exchange policy. It's not hard to imagine some people wanting their wages or hours kept low for this reason. So the Medicaid expansion might have the perverse effect of depressing wages in some cases. If you have low-paid or part-time workers where this issue could arise, you will need to be careful not to harm your employees' situations.

D. DECLINE TO OFFER TO THOSE WITH ACCESS TO PUBLIC COVERAGE

A risky strategy that at least on its face might work would be to decline coverage offers to workers with access to public coverage like Medicaid, Medicare and certain veteran's coverage. Recall that the ShaRP is only triggered when a full-time employee goes to the exchange AND receives a subsidy. People with access to public coverage are not eligible for exchange subsidies. No subsidy, no ShaRP.

It seems this strategy could work, but could be subject to a discrimination claim and if it does not work, could lead to the ShaRP based on the entire workforce. If you consider this strategy at all, make sure to run it by your tax, legal and insurance advisors. In addition, there are business and ethical considerations as well. Some companies might not want to be known for denying health insurance to seniors, needy people, and veterans.

REFERENCES AND FURTHER READING

Here is a short article on the 29er and 49er trend http://thefranchisecounsel.com/2013/03/05/49ers-29ers-and-americas-brave-new-employment-world-under-the-affordable-care-act-aca/

For a good article with various business strategies, see http://www.americanbar.org/newsletter/publications/aba_health_esource_home/aba_health_law_esource_1107_nelson.html.

For some novel, advanced strategies, go to http://www.paulhastings.com/publications-items/details/?id=ECC52A26-8AA5-6986-8B86-FF00008CFFC3.

CHAPTER 21:

CONCLUDING REMARKS

We hope you have found this guidebook useful. We set out to write a short book that would help employers decide what to do as Obamacare takes effect. We conclude with a few remarks about business ethics and strategy.

Employers face an obligation for the wellbeing of their employees. Many employers have felt that providing insurance is an important way of not just attracting good employees, but a way of improving the quality of the lives of their workers and their families. You will have to decide for yourself where your moral compass points when you decide what to do with your organization's health coverage.

As Obamacare takes full effect in 2014 and 2015, we believe the obligation to offer insurance and even the competitive advantage insurance gives in competing for employees will weaken. Employees value employer provided insurance highly because in many cases it is not available or extremely expensive to get otherwise. With the exchanges, that won't be true any more. Because there will be a reasonable alternative to employer-based coverage for your employees, you may be in a better position to drop coverage than if Obamacare had not become law. But then again, you might take the high road and offer insurance anyway.

Another thing to consider is the reaction of customers and protest groups, especially if you decide to drop coverage. Some companies have faced boycott pressures when it became public they were employing the 29er strategy. In addition, there might be potential social pressure and stigma associated with being a "selfish" or "greedy" company who does not offer health insurance. These factors remain to be seen, but you should consider them now.

We also believe Obamacare will have tremendous, unforeseen impacts on the labor market. Industry leaders will likely have substantial influence over practices in their industries. We expect that in some industries the norm will be to offer good insurance packages. Other industries will adopt SHOP as the go-to model, while others might go the self-funding plan route. Still other industries may see the exchanges as good enough and let their employees buy their own policies. We urge you to monitor trends in your industry, particularly watching what leading companies decide to do. If your company is a leading company, keep in mind that your decisions impact not only your workers but probably also those of your competitors as well.

In closing, we wish you the best of luck with your enterprise. Face up to Obamacare and do what is best for your organization and its employees. Reading a book like this is a good first step. Probably the best advice we can give is to not be afraid to get help. Your legal, tax, and insurance advisors have probably been working hard to get up to speed on Obamacare. They are there to help you.

Glossary

Actuarial Value: The percentage of total, average costs that a health insurance plan will cover. For example, where a plan has an actuarial value of 80%, the insured individual will be responsible for 20% of healthcare costs. See http://www.healthcare.gov/glossary/a/acturial.html.

Applicable Large Employer: An employer which, through the course of a calendar year, hires an average of 50 or more full-time or full-time equivalent employees. Sec. 4980H(c)(2); see http://www.gibbonslaw.com/news_publications/articles.php?action=display_publication&publication_id=4110.

Annual Limits: A cap on the benefits an insurance company will pay in a year on behalf of an individual enrolled in a particular health insurance plan. Caps can come in the form of monetary limits or a limit of the number of visits made to a medical facility. See http://www.healthcare.gov/glossary/a/annuallimit.html.

Benchmark Plan: By 2014, each state is required to approve a health-care plan meeting all the minimum essential benefits requirements.

This plan will serve as a model for health insurers in each state. See http://cciio.cms.gov/resources/files/Files2/02172012/ehb-faq-508.pdf.

Common Law Employee: Under judge-made case law, any individual who performs a service or task for another individual (commonly known as an employer) for compensation. The degree of control the employer has over the person determines whether a person is a common law employee or independent contractor. An employee counts towards whether the employer is an applicable large employer and if full-time may be entitled to an offer of health insurance. See http://www.irs.gov/Businesses/Small-Businesses-&-Self-Employed/Employee-(Common-Law-Employee).

Employer Mandate: The requirement that employers must provide health insurance to their full-time employees. Beginning in 2014 (enforcement delayed until 2015), all applicable large employers who do not provide affordable health care coverage will be assessed a penalty if at least one full-time employee qualifies for a premium tax credit and uses it to purchase coverage in the health insurance exchange. Additionally, the law requires employers to provide prescribed health coverage and penalizes some employers who may fail to offer what is defined by the law as "affordable" coverage. See http://www.uschamber.com/health-reform/employer-mandate.

Essential Health Benefits: Beginning in 2014, every health insurance policy will have to provide certain government-defined benefits. See http://www.uhc.com/united_for_reform_resource_center/health_reform_provisions/essential_health_benefits.htm.

Full-time employee: An employee that averages more than 30 hours of work per week in a given month. Section 4980H(c)(4)(A). Further rules attempt to more specifically define a full-time employee.

Full-time equivalent employee: By formula, a group of part-time employees count as full-time employees. For example, two half-time workers count as one full-time worker. Section 4980H(c)(2)(E).

Grandfathered Plan: Health insurance plans in existence prior to March 23rd 2010 that meet the criteria of Section 1251 of PPACA and all other applicable regulations.

Individual Mandate: The requirement that all individuals obtain health insurance or pay a penalty. See http://www.healthreformgps.org/glossary/#G.

Initial Measurement Period: A time period allowing employers to determine "full-time" or "part-time" status of variable-hour and seasonal employees. See http://www.towerswatson.com/en-US/Insights/Newsletters/Americas/health-care-reform-bulletin/2012/guidance-arrives-on-safe-harbor-methods-to-determine-full-time-employee-status.

Leased Employee: A person who provides services (1) to a recipient company pursuant to an agreement between the recipient company and the leasing organization; (2) on a substantially full-time basis; and (3) under the primary direction or control of the recipient company. Leased employees can count as full-time employees under PPACA. See http://www.irs.gov/Retirement-Plans/Employee-Plans-Compliance-Unit-(EPCU)—Completed-Projects—Project-with-Summary-Reports—Leased-Employees.

Lifetime Limits: The upper limit on the amount of benefits that an insurer will pay over the lifetime of an insured individual.

Medicaid: A federal program enacted in 1965 that is funded by the federal and state governments and administered by the states that provides health insurance coverage to certain low-income people.

Medicare: The federal health insurance program for people aged 65 and older, as well as persons with end-stage renal disease and certain persons with disabilities. Medicare covers beneficiaries for hospital, post-hospital extended care, and home health care, as well as a range of medical care services and benefits. Medicare enrollment is generally compulsory for all individuals covered by the Social Security Act.

Obamacare: The common name used to identify the Patient Protection and Affordable Care Act.

Open enrollment period: The time period where people can newly enroll or change their health insurance plan. For most kinds of insurance, open enrollment occurs once per year. Under Obamacare, open enrollment for the exchanges is scheduled to begin October 1, 2013. The states and HHS will announce annual open enrollment periods for 2014 and subsequent years.

Patient Protection and Affordable Care Act (PPACA): The formal name given to House Bill 3590, passed on March 23, 2010. It is commonly referred to as Obamacare or the Affordable Care Act. See http://www.healthreformgps.org/glossary/#G.

Penalty Tax: Because the Supreme Court ruled that the payment required by someone who violates the individual mandate by failing to get insurance is a tax for some purposes and a penalty for other purposes, the government now refers to the tax or penalty as a penalty tax. See http://www.businessinsider.com/how-much-is-the-obamacare-penalty-tax-2012-7.

Qualified Health Benefit Plans (QHBP): Health insurance plans that meet minimum federal insurance-market rules including offering a standard set of services, benefits, and other requirements. See http://www.cigna.com/aboutus/health-care-reform/faqs.

Seasonal Employee: Generally, seasonal employees work during busy seasons, typically the holiday and harvest seasons. The rules under PPACA are extremely uncertain on who qualifies as a seasonal employee.

Self-Funding Plans: Health coverage arrangements under which the plan's sponsor (e.g. an employer, other type of group such as a union or association) chooses to bear the risk for employee or group member health care costs rather than purchasing private insurance to cover all or part of the group's losses. Commonly self-funding plans are combined with a stop-loss insurance policy to cover large claims. See: http://www.healthreformgps.org/glossar/#G.

Shared Responsibility Payment (ShaRP): The penalty an employer who violates the employer mandate must pay. See Sec. 4980H.

Summary of Benefits (SBC): Health insurers and group plans will have to provide an easy-to-understand, universally standard summary about a health plan's benefits and coverage. The new regulation is designed to help the American public better understand and evaluate their health insurance choices. See http://www.healthcare.gov/law/features/rights/sbc/.

Temporary Employee: An employment situation where an employee is expected to remain in a position only for a certain period of time. Temporary employees may have the opportunity to achieve permanent employment status after the time period has lapsed. Temporary workers may also be referred to as seasonal employees or temps. The PPACA rules for temps are complex and uncertain. See http://www.businessdictionary.com/definition/temporary-employment.html

Variable Hour Employee: A new employee where it is not clear whether the employee will be full-time or part-time. The PPACA rules for handling variable hour employees are complex and uncertain. See http://www.cbiz.com/page.asp?pid=10003.

Index

CPSIA information can be obtained at www.ICGtesting.com
Printed in the USA
LVOW07s1502180913

353041LV00016B/872/P